Lord, I Want to Be Whole
Workbook and Journal

Lord, I Want to Be Whole Workbook and Journal

A Personal Prayer Journey

Stormie Omartian

THOMAS NELSON
Since 1798

NASHVILLE   DALLAS   MEXICO CITY   RIO DE JANEIRO   BEIJING

Published in Nashville, Tennessee, by Thomas Nelson, Inc.

All Scripture quotations, unless otherwise indicated, are taken from the New King James Version. Copyright © 1982 by Thomas Nelson, Inc. Used by permission. All rights reserved.

Scripture quotations noted NIV are from the HOLY BIBLE: NEW INTERNATIONAL VERSION. Copyright © 1973, 1978, 1984 by International Bible Society. Used by permission of Zondervan Publishing House. All rights reserved.

Scripture quotations noted NLT are from the *Holy Bible,* New Living Translation, copyright © 1996. Used by permission of Tyndale House Publishers, Inc., Wheaton, Illinois 60189. All rights reserved.

ISBN 10: 0-785-26441-8
ISBN 13: 978-0-785-26441-5

Printed in the United States of America

08 09 10 VG 10 9 8

CONTENTS

STEP SIX: Reject the Pitfalls

STEP SEVEN: Stand Strong

STEPS TO EMOTIONAL HEALTH

When my dad turned ninety, I began to notice a difference in his health. He wasn't necessarily sick, nor did he have a terminal disease such as cancer. He just started losing weight and got very frail; everything seemed to be a real effort for him. I know he felt miserable about that because he had always been so active. By the end of 2001, when he was ninety-three, he seemed to have deteriorated further each time I saw him. At the traditional Christmas dinner at our home, he said he didn't want any pumpkin pie, so I knew something was really wrong then. Dad never would have missed his favorite dessert. He had to leave the celebration immediately after dinner because he was so exhausted.

Two weeks later he got up at 6:30 in the morning, fixed a bowl of cereal, and went back down to his little terrace apartment in my sister's home. Just before my brother-in-law, Louis, left for work at 10:30 A.M., he heard the radio playing in Dad's room. When Louis came home about 3:30 that afternoon, Dad was not upstairs, which was unusual since he was always out and about during the afternoon. Louis went to check on Dad and found him in bed, just as if he were sleeping. The radio was off, so Dad had obviously gone back to bed because he wasn't feeling well.

We held a private family funeral for him—just my sister, Susie; her husband and her three children, Stephanie, Derek, and Matt; and Michael and me and our children, Christopher and Amanda. As we sat in a circle, each one telling a favorite memory of Dad, I realized that I had become completely at peace with my past. I had forgiven my mother for things she had said and done to me over the years and my dad for things he hadn't done to protect me from a mentally ill mother. I had peace with my relationship with my parents. It reminded me that emotional health can be achieved. We are all locked up in some way in our lives, but Jesus has the keys to let us out.

What Is Emotional Health?

Many people look upon their emotional state with resignation: "This is just the way I am." Others believe that one has to be either very spiritual to become more emotionally healthy on their own or very wealthy to be able to afford the best professional help. "Emotional health," one girl told me, "is a remote ideal that many people want but very few people achieve."

My definition of emotional health is having total peace about who you are, what you're doing, and where you're going, both individually and in relationship to those around you. It's feeling totally at peace about the past, the present, and the future of your life. It's knowing that you're in line with God's ultimate purpose for you—and being fulfilled in that.

How about you? In the space below list the moments in your past that give you peace and well-being when remembering them:

Now think about the moments in your past that make you feel agitated and uneasy. List those moments below:

My Devorce, The Feeling of Being run over

Next look at your present. List the moments that give you a feeling of peace and well-being:

Seeing all my Bills being paid. spending Time with Krister

Now look at the moments in the present that make you feel agitated and uneasy. List those moments below: *Insurity in life with Bills, The way people Try everything they can To Try and get me angry.*

Finally, think about the future. What events in the future might make you happy and at peace? List them below: *To See No Debt in my Life, marry The one in my Life that Has Reliested my Ability to Love*

What events in the future might make you afraid and uneasy? List them below. *~~Over~~, Touching Dead Bodies, Asking the one I Love to Marry me Asking For a fathers Blessing - Become Closer with God*

Looking at the lists above, note the two most important events (the ones that made you feel afraid and uneasy) in the past, present, and future that you need to deal with as you read this book:

Past:

1. *Devorce*

2. *~~scribbled out~~*

Present:

1. *Insurity*

2.

Future:

1. *~~scribbled~~ Work*

2.

In contrast to what many people think, emotional health is just as practical and attainable as physical health. If you don't feed your body the right food, you will become ill and die. Spiritually, emotionally, and mentally, you have to be fed and cared for properly, or that part of you gets sick and dies a slow death.

I know. I've come a long way since I was a child, living with a mother who was physically and verbally abusive.

My mother constantly told me, "You're worthless, and you'll never amount to anything." Worse yet, she locked me in a little closet underneath the stairs when I did anything to disturb her.

I had to stay in that closet until she remembered I was there, or when my father returned from work and then she would let me out.

During my growing-up years, my mother's extremely erratic behavior left me with feelings of futility, hopelessness, helplessness, and deep emotional pain. So much so that by the time I was a young woman, I was still locked in a closet—except the boundaries were emotional rather than physical.

I threw myself into anything I thought would help me get free of all that—Eastern religions, occult practices, psychotherapy, unhealthy relationships, and a short, ill-fated marriage. When it became obvious that each of these things fell far short of meeting my desperate needs, I sank deeper into depression. I turned to drugs and alcohol with dangerous frequency in hopes of momentarily transcending this chronic emotional torture.

I wrote about these experiences in my autobiography, *Stormie*. After its publication I was deluged with letters from people telling me of their own emotionally traumatic circumstances.

Many women said, "I just want to be whole. You've shown me for the first time that is possible to be free of emotional pain. But now that I know there is hope for my life, what steps can I take to experience the same healing you've found?"

I knew I needed to put all the information I had on the subject in a book, so I wrote *Lord, I Want to Be Whole*. Now I am adding this workbook and journal so that women can individually—or in a Bible study or Sunday school class—work through their own personal struggles. In this book *you* will be guiding the experience, and I will only be a companion to the process.

We will go through the seven steps to emotional health that I related in *Lord, I Want to Be Whole*, but this time you will be continually assessing your own experience. These steps led to my own healing over thirty years ago—and have kept me emotionally healthy ever since.

Seven Steps to Emotional Health

Your mind and emotions need to be freed from stress, fed properly, exercised, cleansed, nurtured, retrained, exposed to freshness and light, and given rest. Here are the seven steps that helped me to do this in my own life and will lead to emotional and spiritual well-being in your life.

Step One: Release the Past

Confess to God the times you have failed and, by moving in full forgiveness, release the times others have failed you.

Step Two: Live in Obedience

Understand that God's rules are for your benefit and try to the best of your knowledge to live His ways, knowing that every step of obedience brings you closer to total wholeness.

Step Three: Find Deliverance

Recognize who your enemy is and remove yourself from anything that separates you from God or keeps you from becoming all He made you to be.

Step Four: Seek Total Restoration

Refuse to accept less than all God has for you and remember that finding wholeness is an ongoing process.

Step Five: Receive God's Gifts

Acknowledge the gifts God has given you and take the steps necessary to receive them.

Step Six: Reject the Pitfalls

Avoid or get free of the negative traps and deceptions that rob you of life.

Step Seven: Stand Strong

Believe that as long as you stand with God and don't give up, you win.

These seven steps are really natural laws that work for our benefit when we live in harmony with them.

You will be able to do the initial work on each of these steps in a week or so, but making them a permanent part of your life takes longer. However, understanding them with your mind *will* influence the state of your heart, which will affect your emotions and ultimately your entire life.

I have tested this plan repeatedly over the past thirty-plus years, and I have seen these steps operate successfully in my life and the lives of countless others. The plan will be as reliable and consistent as you are in following it.

Right now, agree to set aside twenty minutes a day, five days a week to interact with this workbook. Some women will want to spend even more time as they take these important steps toward emotional and spiritual wholeness.

What You Should Expect in the Next Few Months

Some of the information in the following chapters will seem *familiar*, almost obvious, but don't be deceived by that. The familiar and obvious are often overlooked for just that reason.

Other information will be *unfamiliar*. You've never heard it before. Or if you have heard it, you haven't applied it to your own life.

Still other information will be *uncomfortable*. You may react to it by closing the book or neglecting to work through the workbook process. Believe me, I understand how hard certain steps are, and how difficult their accomplishment seems. But I would be less than helpful if I did not present you with the whole truth. If I left out some of the pieces, you would have an incomplete plan for emotional restoration, and you'd live in frustration trying to find the missing piece. So I'm going to tell it to you as straight as I know how, and it's up to you to choose to accept it. Remember that you do the choosing. God working in you, as you allow Him entrance, makes it happen in your life.

The healing and restoration I found is there for you too. Whether your hurt is from scars from as far back as early childhood or from this week's untimely severing of a precious relationship, you can be whole spiritually and emotionally.

But once you are healed, don't be misled into thinking you will never have a problem again. It just isn't so. Problems are a part of life in this world. You can be devastated by them, or you can meet them head-on and make them work for you.

As I close this chapter I want you to take a second look at your life from a different perspective. Let's go back to my definition of emotional health: having total peace about who you are, what you're doing, and where you're going, both individually and in relationship to those around you.

Think about who you are. Write a description of yourself in the space below. (Be sure to include who you are spiritually and emotionally.)

Do you have total peace about who you are? _____ yes; _X_ no.

If not, mention below the ways you might want to change:

Be more trusting. put more of my Life into god. "All of my Life"

Now think about who you are in relationship to those around you. Write that description in the space below: *Loving, CARing, Friendly Loyal, Trustworthy, Committed*

Are you at peace with who you are in relationship to others?
_____ yes; _✓_ no.

If not, mention below the ways you might want to change in relationship to others: *Be more trusting*

Think about what you're doing. Look back at the past week and month and year. Mention the activities that seem to consume most of your time in the space below:

In the past week . . . *Work*

In the past month . . . *Work*

In the past year . . . *Work*

Are you at peace with what you are doing? _____ yes; _✓_ no.

If not, mention below the ways you might want to change what you are doing in the future:

Give more time to God AND Kristan AND my kids

Now think about what you are doing and how it affects those around you. Write that description in the space below:

Are you at peace with the way you affect those around you? _____ yes; _____ no.

If not, mention below the ways you might want to change the way you affect others:

Finally, think about where you are going. Write a description below of what you anticipate your future to be:

Are you at peace with where you seem to be going? _____ yes; _____ no.

If not, mention below the ways you would like to make changes that would affect your future:

Now think about where you are going in relationship to those around you. How does it affect them? Write a description in the space below:

Are you at peace with where you are going in relationship to others? _____ yes; _____ no.

If not, mention in the space below how you might want to change that:

Throughout our journey together the Bible will be our constant companion. During some steps you will look up passages and interact with them. When you get to Step Six—Reject the Pitfalls—the Bible passages will be there for you so you can copy them onto an index card or Xerox that page and then put the Scriptures on a mirror or place them in your purse for personal reference.

You will also be journaling your prayers and life experiences throughout this process. (There are some blank journal pages at the end of this book so you can begin the process in the days ahead.) And you will be observing the lives of some familiar people in the Bible. Many of these people had the same faults—and suffered the same problems—we do. The way the Lord guided them will be a path you can follow in your journey to emotional and spiritual well-being.

Finally, do not forget that emotional and spiritual wholeness is a process that involves changing habits of thinking, feeling, or acting. These seven steps are not a quick fix, but a permanent way to transform your inner being.

God's Promises of Healing

Look up the following Scriptures and write them in the spaces below.

    Deuteronomy 32:39

    God promises that _____.
    Jeremiah 3:22

    God promises that _____.
    Jeremiah 30:17

    God promises that _____.
    Luke 4:18

    Jesus promises that _____.
    James 5:13–15

    This passage promises that _____.
    It directs me to _____.

Step 1
Release the Past

Confess to God the times you have failed and,
by moving in full forgiveness, release the times
others have failed you.

THE FOUNDATION OF CONFESSION

When I was feeling desperate about my emotional health, I called to make an appointment with a psychologist. The assistant who answered my request asked, "What is the nature of the problem?"

When I said I'd rather talk with the doctor, she persisted. "I preview all cases," she said. "I can't make an appointment for you unless I know the nature of your problem."

I told her about my depression, which I felt was caused by being raised by an abusive mother.

Her answer astonished me. "It is our policy that we do not accept the story of child abuse."

I was devastated. Where could I go for help? I was suicidal. Thankfully, a friend who knew I was emotionally spent took me to meet her pastor, Jack Hayford, at The Church on the Way. He told me about the wholeness and peace I could find by receiving Jesus into my life.

This "Jesus thing" sounded like a long shot, but with suicide as the only alternative I could see, I had nothing to lose. And if Pastor Jack was right, I had everything to gain.

After I made this commitment to accept Christ as Savior, I felt hope for the first time I could remember. As it turned out, this was the beginning point of my healing. I started attending The Church on the Way, reading the Bible, and praying every day. I even found the man I would marry sitting behind me in church one Sunday morning.

If you haven't made a similar commitment yourself, just say, "Jesus, I acknowledge You this day. I believe You are the Son of God as You say You are. Although it's hard to comprehend a love so great, I believe You laid down your life for me so that I might have life eternally and abundantly now. I ask You to forgive me for not living Your way. I need You to help me become all You created me to be. Come into my life and fill me with Your Holy Spirit. Let all the death in me be crowded out by the power of Your presence and this day turn my life into a new beginning."

If you don't feel comfortable with this prayer, then talk to Jesus as you would to a good friend. Confess you've made some mistakes. Tell Him you can't live without Him. Ask Him to forgive you and come into your heart. Tell Him you receive Him as Lord, and thank Him for His eternal life and forgiveness.

After Michael Omartian and I were married, I felt safe enough to tell him about my early childhood. He insisted that I see a counselor at The Church on the Way. Mary Anne would become God's instrument to help me release my past.

The Foundation of Confession

When Mary Anne and I met together, I admitted, "I have these depressions that happen frequently, like emotional blackouts that last as long as two weeks at a time."

Without my mentioning my past, Mary Anne immediately asked, "Tell me about your childhood, Stormie."

After the response I'd received from that psychologist's office, I was truly blessed to hear Mary Anne confront the problem I knew was causing me distress. In the next half hour I told her more about my past than I had ever related to anyone. I revealed my anger toward my mother.

Then Mary Anne said very directly, "You have bondage, Stormie, and you need deliverance."

I have what? I need what? I wondered.

Mary Anne must have read my expression, because she quickly added, "It's nothing to be afraid of. Bondage is the oppression that comes upon us when we don't live the way we're supposed to. Deliverance breaks that oppression."

She told me to go home and write down every sin God brought to my mind. "Ask God to help you remember each incident, and as you write it down say, 'God, I confess this before You and ask Your forgiveness.'"

I was confused. "I thought I was forgiven of all my sins when I received Jesus," I said politely.

Mary Anne explained that Jesus took all that we had coming to us, which is death, and in return He gave us all that He had coming to Him, which is eternal life. Receiving Him meant being free from this death grip. However, the bondage that accompanied each of our sins must be severed through confession.

I knew that the word *sin* is an old archery term, meaning "to miss the bull's-eye." Anything off the center of God's best and perfect will for our lives is sin. In fact, 1 John 5:17 says "All unrighteousness is sin." That takes in a lot of territory!

The Weight of Unconfessed Sin

Chuck Colson knew the pain of unconfessed sin—and repenting of these sins turned his life around. I met Chuck about fifteen years ago when he asked me to be a part of the Prison Fellowship team that was going into a California prison. As I was speaking to the women that day, one woman began running up and down the aisle handing pieces of toilet paper to different women. At first Colson said he couldn't understand what this woman was doing. Then he realized that she was passing tissues to the women who were crying.

This was really touching for me since I was talking about God's restoration and His plan for emotional healing, the same material in this book.

I have always admired Chuck Colson for what he has done through his Prison Fellowship ministry for people who are incarcerated. He helps prisoners realize that there is hope for their lives—and that has always been my goal too. Chuck has come a long way from the days when he was known as President Richard Nixon's "hatchet man."

This change began one night when he visited the home of Tom Phillips. Tom knew the pressure Colson was under at the time: the Watergate scandal had broken and although Chuck Colson had not yet been indicted, he knew this was a possibility.

At this meeting Tom shared his belief in Christ as Savior, and then he read excerpts from *Mere Christianity* by C. S. Lewis to Colson. "There is one vice of which no man in the world is free . . . and of which hardly any people, except Christians, ever imagine they are guilty . . . The vice I am talking of is Pride or Self-Conceit."

Colson felt naked and unclean as Tom read these words. He felt the weight of unconfessed sin. "I was exposed, unprotected, for Lewis's words were describing me.

"Just as a man about to die is supposed to see flash before him, sequence by sequence, the high points of his life, so, as Tom's voice read on that August evening, key events in my life paraded before me as if projected on a screen. Things I hadn't thought about in years—my graduation speech at prep school—being 'good enough' for the Marines—my first marriage, into the 'right' family—sitting on the Jaycees' dais while civic leader after civic leader praised me as the outstanding young man of Boston—then to the White House—the clawing and straining for status and position—'Mr. Colson, the President is calling—Mr. Colson, the President wants to see you right away.'

"Now, sitting there on the dimly lit porch, my self-centered past was washing over me in waves. It was painful. Agony. Desperately I tried to defend myself. What about my sacrifices for government service, the giving up of a big income, putting my stocks into a blind trust? The truth, I saw in an instant, was that I'd wanted the position in the White House more than I'd wanted money. There was no sacrifice . . .

"In those brief moments while Tom read, I saw myself as I never had before. And the picture was ugly."[1]

Colson was feeling the weight of unconfessed sin.

As he left Tom Phillips's home that night, Colson's eyes began to fill with tears. At first he was angry with himself. "What kind of weakness is this?" he said to nobody. Then he gave into his sorrow. "I forgot about machismo, about pretenses, about fears of being weak. And as I did, I began to experience a wonderful feeling of being released. Then came the strange sensation that water was not only running down my cheeks, but surging through my whole body as well, cleansing and cooling as it went. They weren't tears of sadness and remorse, nor of joy—but somehow, tears of relief."[2]

Chuck Colson's feeling of relief was God's way of establishing a relationship with him. And it's God's way of establishing a relationship with us as well.

When sin is left unconfessed, a wall goes up between you and God. Even though the sin may have stopped, it will still weigh you down. As I followed Mary Anne's instructions and listed my sins, I realized that unconfessed sin is like carrying around heavy bags of garbage. The heavier they get, the weaker we become—until we are crippled under the weight of it all. When I confessed my sins, I actually felt the weight being lifted.

Often we fail to see ourselves as responsible for certain actions. These are the hidden sins. For example, while it's not your fault that someone abused you, your reaction to it now is your responsibility. I was justified in my anger toward my mother, but I still had to confess it because it missed the mark of what God had for me.

Take a moment to do this type of introspection. Look back into your childhood and then your youth, as Chuck Colson did. Think about the years after that time. Take several days to do this, adding to the list when the Holy Spirit brings something to mind.

To begin the process, you may want to check below the areas in which you might have sinned. These are some of the pitfalls I will discuss in Step Six. Have you been guilty of falling into any of these sins?

_____ Anger

_____ Criticism

_____ Envy

_____ Lust

_____ Lying

_____ Pride

_____ Rebellion against God

Be specific about any ways you have sinned in these or other areas during your childhood, your youth, and your adulthood. If you need extra space, use the journal pages at the back of this book.

Moments in my childhood:

Moments in my youth:

Moments in adulthood:

Look back over this list and as you do so, say, "God, I confess this before You and ask Your forgiveness."

Now think again. Ask God to reveal any hidden sins to you. List them in the space below and as you do so say, "God, I confess this before You and ask Your forgiveness."

Finally, write a prayer in the space below, asking God to forgive you for all the sins He has brought to your mind.

Then hear Him speak these words back to you:

> "Though your sins are like scarlet,
> They shall be as white as snow;
> Though they are red like crimson,
> They shall be as wool." (Isa. 1:18)

Now tear these pages out of the workbook and burn them. Your sins have been forgiven.

For confession to work, repentance must go along with it.

Turning Your Back on These Sins

Repentance literally means "a change of mind." It means that we turn our backs on these sins, walk away, and vow never to do these things again. As we confess and repent we are saying, "This is my fault. I'm sorry about it, and I'm not going to do it anymore."

After Chuck Colson recognized his sins and repented of them, he turned his life around. Sometime following his conversion, he agreed to speak at an annual prayer breakfast in a small Michigan community. Toward the end of his talk, he decided to mention the indictments the Watergate prosecutors had entered against him so the people at the prayer breakfast could know the truth of his innocence and better accept his testimony.

"I know in my own heart," he said, "that I am innocent of *many* of the charges . . ."

Colson stopped for a moment as he realized he had said the word *many*, not *all*; thankfully, reporters at the occasion didn't pick up on his slip since he quickly corrected himself.

But Chuck felt this slip of the tongue might be God's voice: "Many, but not *all* the charges, Chuck!"[3]

In the next days Chuck Colson decided he would plead guilty to the charge of disseminating derogatory information to the press about Daniel Ellsberg, the man who had leaked the Pentagon Papers to the media.

Some people thought Colson's sentence would be minimal. After all, an offense of this nature had never been considered a crime before. Yet

Judge Gerhard Gesell pronounced a sentence of one to three years and a fine of five thousand dollars.[4]

Colson turned his back on his sins—and took responsibility for his actions, which is what we must do. We will talk further about how to avoid these sins in Step Six, Reject the Pitfalls. Right now, determine that you will not go back there again.

How do you know if you have turned your back on these sins?

Chuck Colson found that he reacted differently to situations and to people whom he had previously disliked—like John Dean, who had told the inside story of the Watergate cover-up to the authorities. "Remarkable things were happening inside me," he said. "I felt less of the old animosity and bitterness toward my adversaries. At a dinner party in October with old White House friends, I found myself suddenly uncomfortable when the others began to attack John Dean.

"'He's got to live with himself,' I responded mildly."[5]

Look for what God is going to do for you in the days ahead, now that you have been relieved of the burden of unconfessed sin.

Confession

Look up the Scriptures below as you think about your sins and confess them to God.

Proverbs 28:13

1 John 1:9–10

Psalm 32:1–5

James 5:16

Mark 4:12

2 Corinthians 2:10

1 John 2:12

As you think about your sins, you might adopt the attitude of King David when he went before the Lord: "For I will declare my iniquity; I will be in anguish over my sin" (Psalm 38:18).

3

THE FOUNDATION OF ONGOING FORGIVENESS

*F*orgiveness is a two-way street. God forgives you for the sins you admitted in the last chapter—and you, in turn, forgive others (and yourself, which is sometimes the hardest). For me, that meant forgiving my mother.

Mary Anne told me that I didn't have to feel forgiveness for my mother. "Forgiveness is something you do out of obedience to the Lord because He has forgiven you."

I soon learned, however, that unforgiveness as deeply rooted as mine toward my mother must be unraveled, one layer at a time. This was especially true for me, since my mother's verbal abuse only continued to increase in intensity as the years went by. I had to learn to take charge of my will and deliberately say, "Lord, my desire is to forgive my mother. Help me to forgive her completely."

During the next years, I did this more often than I can begin to count. One day as I was again asking God to give me a forgiving heart, I felt led to pray, "Lord, help me to have a heart like Yours for my mother."

Almost immediately I had a vision of her I had never seen before. She was a beautiful, fun-loving, gifted woman who bore no resemblance to the person I knew. That's the way God had made her.

Unfortunately, the pieces of her past had destroyed that vision: the tragic and sudden death of her mother when she was eleven; the suicide of her beloved uncle and foster father a few years later; her feelings of abandonment, guilt, bitterness, and unforgiveness, which contributed to her emotional and mental illness. Suddenly I no longer hated my mother. I felt sorry for her instead—and I forgave her.

Stairway to Wholeness

Once we are forgiven and released from everything we've ever done wrong, how can we refuse to obey God when He asks us to forgive others? Easy! We focus our thoughts on the person who has wronged us rather than on the God who makes all things right.

Take a moment now to focus on God, your Heavenly Father, by praising God as the psalmist does:

> The LORD is my rock and my fortress and my deliverer;
> My God, my strength, in whom I will trust;
> My shield and the horn of my salvation, my stronghold.
> I will call upon the LORD, who is worthy to be praised;
> So shall I be saved from my enemies . . .
> The LORD lives!
> Blessed be my Rock!
> Let the God of my salvation be exalted. (Ps. 18:2–3,46)

The God of your salvation will help you forgive those who have harmed you. He has the grace and the power to do so. The most important thing to remember about forgiveness is that forgiveness doesn't make the other person right; it makes you free.

Scripture makes this very important point: "He who loves his brother abides in the light, and there is no cause for stumbling in him. But he who hates his brother is in darkness and walks in darkness, and does not know where he is going, because the darkness has blinded his eyes" (1 John 2:10–11).

Pastor Jack Hayford said something that affected me profoundly: "When you hate your parents, you grow up to hate yourself, because what you see of them in yourself, you will despise."

If you have a grudge against one of your parents, fill in the appropriate space below:

"My _____ hit me when I did something wrong—and sometimes when I didn't. His/her anger was abusive."

"My _____ was always criticizing me. I never seemed to do anything right."

"My _____ never showed any affection for me."

Now think about yourself. Do you have a tendency to be like your mother or father in this way, or do you repeat any other offense your parent committed toward you? If so, mention it below.

Now write a prayer, asking God for forgiveness for this sin.

Finally, think about those who have harmed you. List any persons in the space below and mention what they have done to you.

I can't forgive _____ because . . .

1.

2.

3.

As you think about these people, hear God speaking to you through the Scriptures. Place your name in the blank below:

Let all bitterness, wrath, anger, clamor, and evil speaking be put away from you, _____, with all malice. And be kind to one another, tenderhearted, forgiving one another, even as God in Christ forgave you, _____. (Eph. 4:31–32)

For me, forgiving others meant forgiving my mother. For Chuck Colson, it meant forgiving those who were witnesses for the United States government in the Watergate scandal: John Dean and Jeb Magruder.

Both of these men would join Chuck Colson as residents of Holabird Prison. And Chuck had reason to resent them: "During the first days of the Ervin hearings, anger would boil up inside me at the mention of his [John Dean's] name."

Colson wondered if he would still feel that way when he first saw Dean in prison. "As I grappled with Christ's admonition not only to forgive but love my enemies, the anger inside me seemed to leave. The forgiveness part was not too difficult. In fact, I became aware of a gut-level admiration of John's courage in pitting himself against the awesome power of the presidency. But to love John, that was not so easy."[1]

John Dean arrived at Holabird Prison one night, surrounded by marshals. He was supposed to be sequestered in his room at all times.

When one of the inmates declared, "He'll go bananas!" Colson felt his last barrier against John Dean break down.

Later that night when he came face to face with Dean, Colson stuck out his hand and said, "Whatever's happened in the past, John, let's forget it. If there's any way I can help you, let me know."

Although the federal marshal quickly separated the two inmates, some old wounds were healed in that moment. And Colson later learned that Dean's belief in God had been strengthened by Watergate, just as Colson's had. This was the beginning of a new relationship.[2]

Jeb Magruder had also found a new faith. On Christmas Eve of 1974, four Watergate prisoners—the two government witnesses, Dean and Magruder, and the two presidential defenders, Colson and Herb

Kalmbach—met together to read the Scriptures about the birth of Christ. These men, who had been archenemies in the past, had become Christian brothers who had truly forgiven each other.

In my own experience I've found that the best way to turn anger, bitterness, hatred, and resentment for someone into love is to pray for that person. God softens your heart when you do. Take each person on your list and pray the prayer I prayed:

> "Lord, my desire is to forgive _____. Help me to forgive him (or her) completely."

Then ask God to help you see this person as He sees him or her. Pray, "Lord, help me to have a heart like Yours for _____."

Go through this exercise for everyone on your list on page 25. Think of how God might see each person. Envision that in your mind and write about it below.

1.

2.

3.

Learn what you can about each person's past, which might help you to understand his or her current behavior.

A friend of mine experienced an epiphany about her alcoholic father, who also suffered from manic depression. She was working with a psychiatrist on a mental health project, and they were talking about bipolar disorder (another name for manic depression). The psychiatrist said, "Years ago when there was no Librium, people with bipolar disorder tried to medicate themselves with alcohol."

My friend was heartsick as she thought of her poor dad trying to overcome a genetic disorder over which he had no control. She was quickly able to forgive him for all the pain his alcoholism had caused her, her mom, and her sister.

Write a prayer below, asking God to help you completely forgive the people you mentioned above.

Remember, God is the only one who knows the whole story of their lives, and therefore we never have the right to judge. Scripture says, "Judge not, that you be not judged" (Matt. 7:1).

You will know that the work of forgiveness is complete when you can honestly say you want God's best for everyone on your list.

Finally, you need to work through this same procedure with two others in mind: yourself and God.

Forgiving Yourself and God

Some of us feel guilty about not being what we think we should be. Instead of beating ourselves up for that, we need to be merciful.

Write a prayer below, asking God to help you forgive yourself for not being perfect. And thank God that He is making you into all that He created you to be.

Now ask God to help you see yourself as He sees you. Pray, "Lord, help me to have a heart like Yours for myself."

Think of how God might see you. Envision that in your mind and describe it below:

Then think about your past. What events have contributed to the person you are today? (This is not a time to cast blame on persons you forgave in the exercise above. Instead, it's a moment to better understand your own behavior and help you to forgive yourself.) List those events in the space below:

With those events in mind say, "I forgive you, _____ [inserting your name in the blank space]. You have done the best you can. Now, with God's help, you will do even better."

Then write a prayer in the space below, asking God to walk with you in the days ahead, guiding you so that you can avoid making these mistakes in the future.

Besides forgiving others and yourself, you must also check to see if you need to forgive God. If you sense that you are mad at Him, say so:

"God, I've been upset with You ever since _____."

Be honest. For instance, "I've been upset with You ever since my husband died" or "I've been upset with You ever since we learned that my son (daughter) has a drug problem."

Release the hurt and let yourself cry. Tears are freeing and healing. Then write a prayer below, confessing your anger and asking God to forgive you. Finally, tell Him that you no longer hold that offense against Him.

Without forgiveness we cannot release the past. Don't let unforgiveness keep you from the healing, joy, and restoration God has for you.

And remember that our God is a God of the miraculous. Chuck Colson received a special blessing after the other three Watergate conspirators—Dean, Magruder, and Kalmbach—were released from prison and Colson was still behind bars.

On Tuesday, January 28, 1975, Representative Al Quie called. He told Colson that he and others had signed a letter to President Gerald Ford, appealing for mercy. Then he said, "There's an old statute someone told me about. I'm going to ask the president if I can serve the rest of your term for you."

Colson was amazed. Quie was the sixth-ranking Republican in the House of Representatives and one of the most respected public figures in Washington. And three other men—Doug Coe, Graham Purcell, and Harold Hughes—were also going to make the same statement.

"It was almost more than I imagined possible," Chuck Colson said, "this love of one man for another.

"It was that night in the quiet of my room that I made the total surrender, completing what had begun in Tom Phillips's driveway eighteen long months before: 'Lord, if this is what it is all about,' I said, 'then I thank You. I praise You for leaving me in prison, for letting them take away my license to practice law . . . I praise You for giving me Your love through these men, for being God, for just letting me walk with Jesus.'"[3]

Just three days after his friends' remarkable offer and Colson's complete surrender of his situation to God, the judge ordered an early release for Colson because of family problems that had arisen.

Without forgiveness we can't release the past. Don't let unforgiveness keep you from the healing, joy, and restoration God has for you.

God's Heart for Forgiveness

Look up the following Scriptures to find God's desire for forgiveness. Write that desire in the spaces below.

2 Corinthians 2:5–7

Ephesians 4:32

Colossians 3:12–13

Psalm 130:3–4

2 Corinthians 2:10

Step 2

Live in Obedience

Understand that God's rules are for your benefit,
and try to live His ways to the best of your ability,
knowing that every step of obedience brings you
closer to total wholeness.

Stepping into Obedience

A few months after my first counseling session with Mary Anne, I still lived on an emotional roller coaster. Oh, my life was far more stable then ever before, but I still yearned for peace.

One morning I read these words in the Bible: "Why do you call Me 'Lord, Lord,' and not do the things which I say?" (Luke 6:46). The passage went on to explain that anyone who hears the words of the Lord and does not put them into practice is building a house with no foundation. When the storm comes, it will collapse and be completely destroyed.

Could it be that I'm getting blown over and destroyed by every wind of circumstance that comes my way because I'm not doing what the Lord says to do in some area? I wondered. I knew I had laid a strong foundation by giving my life to the Lord, but it appeared that this foundation could only be stabilized and protected through my obedience.

Are you feeling as I was feeling? Check the statements below that apply to you:

_____ "I am devastated by what other people say to me."

_____ "I view every hint of trouble as the end of the world."

_____ "I wonder if I will ever be able to go through the normal occurrences of life without being traumatized by them."

_____ "I am feeling like a failure."

If you checked any of those statements, you are feeling as unstable I was that day.

In the next days I searched the Bible for more information, and every place I turned I read about the rewards of obeying God, passages like "Blessed are those who hear the word of God and keep it!" (Luke 11:28).

And the more I read, the more I saw the link between obedience and the presence of God. "If anyone loves Me, he will keep My word; and My Father will love him, and We will come to him and make Our home with him" (John 14:23).

I also saw a definite connection between obedience and the love of God. "If anyone obeys his Word, God's love is truly made complete in him" (1 John 2:5 NIV). According to the Bible, God doesn't stop loving us if we *don't* obey. But we are unable to feel or enjoy that love fully if we're not living as God intended us to live.

The more I read about obedience, the more I realized that my disobedience of God's directives could explain why nothing happened when I prayed the same prayers over and over. The Bible says, "One who turns away his ear from hearing the law, / Even his prayer is an abomination" (Prov. 28:9).

If I'm not obeying God in some way, then I shouldn't expect to get my prayers answered, I thought.

And that's a disastrous thought for any of us.

Christ Himself lived in obedience to the Father, even accepting the brutal death of the cross for our sins. Scripture tells us: "And being found in appearance as a man, He humbled Himself and became obedient to the point to death, even the death of the cross" (Phil. 2:8).

Write a prayer in the space below, telling God that you don't want to be someone who collapses when trouble comes your way. Let Him know that you really want to obey His commandments and ask Him to show you, as you walk through this step, any way in which you have disobeyed Him.

Scriptural Truths about the Significance of Obedience

Look up these Scripture passages and write them in the spaces below. Put a star next to the ones that are most significant to you. Then answer the questions below.

Deuteronomy 11:26–28

Who receives the blessing in these verses?

_____

Who receives the curse? _____

Which side would you like to be on?

Acts 5:29–32

Whom is Peter speaking to here? _____

Was he putting himself in danger to assert that he would obey God rather than men? Why?

Are you willing to do the same?

Romans 6:15–22

What is the end of those who are slaves to sin?

_____

What is the end of those who live in obedience?

_____

5

TAKE CHARGE OF YOUR MIND

I was always afraid that I would inherit my mother's predisposition to mental illness, so when I started having some frightening thoughts after I was in counseling with Mary Anne, I told her, "Sometimes I feel like I'm losing my mind."

She said I was being mentally oppressed, which is quite different from being mentally ill. "You've been delivered from major oppression, but you still must choose to let the mind of Christ control you. You've started allowing yourself to listen to whatever thoughts come into your mind."

I grew up with a mother whose every wild thought controlled her, so it had never occurred to me that I could choose my thoughts.

"The Bible makes it clear we are not to conform to the world's way of thinking," Mary Anne said. "It says we are to renew our minds by taking 'captive every thought to make it obedient to Christ.' God has also made clear what we are to allow into our minds: 'Whatever is true, whatever is noble, whatever is right, whatever is pure, whatever is lovely, whatever is admirable—if anything is excellent or praiseworthy.'"

Mary Anne told me I had to resist these frightening thoughts in Jesus' name.

Immediately I set about doing just that. Whenever upsetting thoughts came into my mind, I said aloud, "I will not be controlled by negative thoughts. God has not given me a spirit of fear. He has given me a sound mind. I have the mind of Christ and I refuse any thoughts that are not of the Lord."

We have to choose daily to allow the mind of Christ to be in us and to allow the wisdom of God to guide us.

What Is Your State of Mind?

It's good to evaluate your state of mind frequently to see if your thoughts are in line with the Lord's. Stop now and take an inventory of your thoughts by checking the statements below that apply to you:

_____ "My thoughts make me feel sad, depressed, lonely, or hopeless."

_____ "My thoughts cause me to be angry, bitter, or unforgiving."

_____ "My thoughts cause me to feel self-hatred and self-doubt."

_____ "My thoughts bring feelings of anxiety or fear."

_____ "I often think of negative memories."

_____ "I sometimes think of immoral sexual images."

_____ "I rarely think of positive things."

If you answered yes to any of these questions, you are living with needless torment, and it's time to take charge of your mind. Scripture says, "For the word of God is living and active . . . it judges the thoughts and attitudes of the heart. Nothing in all creation is hidden from God's sight. Everything is uncovered and laid bare before the eyes of him to whom we must give account" (Heb. 4:12–13 NIV).

I've found that the best way to control my thoughts is to control my outside influences. For instance, how many soap operas have you watched that have made you feel hopeful, energetic, and uplifted? Not many, I'm sure. That's because whatever goes into your mind affects your emotions. You have to be specific about what you allow into your mind and truly take *every* thought captive.

Write a prayer below, asking God to help you uncover the influences that are causing you to feel as you do. Ask Him to reveal any negative thinking and set you free from it.

Now take an inventory of the influences you are allowing to affect your thoughts by checking the statements below that apply to you.

_____ "I watch television programs that glorify ungodly activity."

_____ "I go to movies that make me feel fearful, uneasy, or unclean."

_____ "I enjoy novels with sexual content."

_____ "I sometimes look at pornographic material."

_____ "I tell or enjoy off-color jokes."

_____ "I see videos that do not glorify God."

If you checked any of these statements, you are allowing your mind to be polluted by the world. If it's not of God, it will make your heart numb to what *is* of God.

Now analyze your thoughts about past events. Do you allow unpleasant memories to run over and over in your mind? If so, list those thoughts below:

Then go through the above list, putting those memories in God's hands. Take each thought and lift it up to Him. Then refuse to think about that incident the next time your mind wanders that way. Unless you are trying to remember them for the specific purpose of being healed or set free, don't let your mind play continuous reruns.

King David knew how much our minds control our thoughts. And he knew that God was aware of our thoughts. In Psalm 139 he said:

> O LORD, You have searched me and known me . . .
> You understand my thought afar off.
> You comprehend my path and my lying down,
> And are acquainted with all my ways . . .
> You have hedged me behind and before,
> And laid Your hand upon me. (vv. 1–3,5)

I really appreciate the promise of this psalm. If my thoughts are aligned with God's, He will put a protective hedge around me. He will lay a hand on my shoulder. I echo David's cry: "Such knowledge is too wonderful for me" (Ps. 139:6).

Be willing to guard your mind so you can receive this blessing.

Tactics of War

The main weapon in mental warfare is to deliberately feed your mind with God's truth and power. Fill your mind with His Word as you work through the different steps in our journey together. Seek out Christian books and magazines. Play Christian music in your home and your car. Put on worship music and turn it loud enough to drown out the negative voices in your mind.

Some movies, music, books, and television programs may not be saying "Jesus is Lord," but they are based on Christian principles and have a Christian spirit behind them. Seek such programs out. And if you are listening to a program that is negative or immoral, turn it off.

Vow to keep yourself free of these influences by writing your name in the blank within the Scripture passage below:

> And do not be conformed to this world, but be transformed by the renewing of your mind, that you, _____, may prove what is that good and acceptable and perfect will of God. (Rom. 12:2)

People Whose Focus Is on the World

Scripture is very clear about the importance of our thoughts. Look up the passages below and write them in the spaces provided. Ask yourself if this is how you would like to be perceived.

Genesis 6:5–6

Proverbs 15:26

Romans 1:21

Ephesians 4:17–18

People Whose Focus Is on God's Laws

Both King David in the Old Testament and the apostle Paul in the New Testament are very clear about the importance of our thoughts. Look up the passages below and write the Scriptures in the spaces provided.

1 Chronicles 28:9

2 Corinthians 10:5

6

Say No to Sexual Immorality

The first time I saw Mary Anne for counseling, she asked me to go home and list my sins. "It's especially important to include every sexual sin you have ever committed."

How embarrassing, I thought. My desperate need for love, approval, and closeness had been so strong that I'd fallen into one wrong relationship after another. It would be mortifying to tell her about all that.

I was grateful when Mary Anne added, "You don't have to go into any detail. Just put down the name, confess your involvement, and ask God to restore you."

Sex As a Soul Tie

Sexual immorality is having sex with anyone to whom you are not married. People are usually sexually immoral because they either believe there is nothing wrong with it, or they are so in need of closeness, love, and affirmation, they don't have the power to say no.

But sex outside of marriage will never be the committed, sacrificial, unconditional love we really need. Sexual immorality is not just a physical encounter; it invades the soul. Sexual joining unites one person with another. When the relationship is broken, a part of the personality of each person is chipped away. Many such involvements cause many chips. By the time the person finds the one she's supposed to be with, she is so fragmented that she doesn't have a whole person to offer.

Sexual immorality scars our souls and damages our emotions more severely than any other disobedience. The road back from such devastation to the inner person is also slower because the fragmentation of the soul is deeper than any caused by other sins. The Bible says, "He who commits sexual immorality sins against his own body" (1 Cor. 6:18).

I know how difficult this step of obedience is, especially for someone who is emotionally needy or who has suffered hurt, rejection, or a lack of love. Fortunately, we have a God who understands how difficult it is. All He asks is that we have a heart that says, "I want to do what's right. God, help me to do it."

How about you? Have you sinned in this area? If so, do as Mary Anne asked me to do. Write the person's name in the space below, then write a short prayer, asking God to forgive you for this sin. Then ask Him to help you remain pure in the future.

Now, tear this page out of the workbook after you have finished this chapter. The sin is gone, forgotten in the heavenly places.

Step Six, Reject the Pitfalls, is near the end of this process to wholeness. At that time we will deal with the possibility that you may be tempted by lust in the future. You have confessed your past sexual sins to God; those sins are forgiven. Step Six will help you to continue to walk in God's ways.

When It Wasn't Your Fault

If you feel tainted by sexual impurity because of acts that were not your choice, God wants you to be released from the burden of them. In his book *Pain and Pretending,* Rich Buhler tells of people who have been sexually abused as children. One person was a middle-aged woman named Marion who described her molestation at the age of four.

"My family was visiting my uncle's farm for Christmas," she said. "I was standing alone in a small orchard near my uncle's barn when my grandfather took my arm abruptly and forcibly took me into a rear door of the barn. I was scared from the moment he touched me because he was being so rough. What happened inside the barn was so frightening and my grandfather's actions were so abusive that I was terrorized. I will always remember the look on his face. The memory of it has tormented me for a lifetime!"[1]

Unfortunately, hundreds of thousands of women and men share some version of this story. In his book Rich Buhler helps these victims work through a season of recovery by facing the truth of what happened to them. These steps can also be beneficial to many of us as we attempt to understand our pasts.

One of the first steps is to face the hidden areas of our lives. A tool that Buhler uses is journaling. He suggests some categories of information that are important to the season of recovery.

Memories

"Start by constructing a history of your childhood as you remember it," Buhler says. "Draw simple floor plans of the houses or churches or schools that were important to your childhood. Try to recall the names of friends, neighbors, or family members and what significance they had (or did not have) in your life. Reflect on how you felt about those around you or how they seemed to feel about you. Pay special attention to what I call the 'branding experiences,' those events in life that helped you form your opinions of yourself. Pay particular attention to anything that was painful or that seemed to involve loss."[2]

Take time now to do just this. Think about a specific house or church or school that was important in your childhood. Draw a floor plan of it in the space below:

Now recall the names of friends, aquaintances, or family members at that time and how they felt about you—and your feelings toward them.

Name	Their feelings toward you	Your feelings toward them
1.		
2.		
3.		
4.		

Think about these people again. What significance did they have in your life?

Name	Significance in your life
1.	
2.	
3.	
4.	

Finally, think about your "branding experiences," those events that shaped your opinions of yourself. Pay particular attention to anything that was painful or that seemed to involve loss. Buhler says, "Even though the majority of deeply hurting people are victims of abuse, not all destruction has been caused by abuse. Some people experienced the death of a parent or some other important person early in life, or have spent a lifetime trying to overcome the devastation of a learning disability or a serious childhood illness. Still others have been deeply affected by the divorce of parents or from growing up in the home of an alcoholic (which frequently does involve abuse)."[3]

Think about your own life in light of Rich Buhler's comments and note your branding experiences in the spaces below:

Branding Experience One

Branding Experience Two

Branding Experience Three

Buhler suggests that you also try to assemble facts from sources other than your own memories.

Facts and Other People's Memories

Record the memories here of your sisters and brothers, for instance. Or family, friends, or neighbors. How do they remember those times?

Sometimes these memories will comfort and reassure you. Other times they will help you realize that your own memories may be distorted or embellished. That's equally important. Be honest about what other people's memories have told you. List your thoughts about that below:

Insights

Rich Buhler has found that as people think about their lives, their pain, and their desires, they have deeper insights into what happened to them. For instance, you may write, "Today I realized my father didn't hate me as much as I thought." Write your insights below as they occur to you now and during the next week.

Buhler also says that he cannot overemphasize the importance of allowing yourself to cry as you come in touch with some painful feelings.

Tears

Southern California psychologist Dr. Mark Johnson once told Rich Buhler about a patient of his who had never cried about her pain. She said, "I think I finally understand why it is so hard for me to shed any tears over this. You see, I still can't believe that it wasn't my fault, and if I were to really let myself cry, it would be admitting my innocence."

"She was right," Buhler says. And that's why Buhler encourages people to write and talk about what's bothering them.[4]

Stop a moment now and imagine those difficult times in your life, your branding experiences. You might allow yourself to relive them. Then give yourself time to fully express your feelings. *Remember, tears are healing.*

One of the final steps in Buhler's season of recovery is forgiveness.

Forgiveness

If this person or persons is one of the people you listed in chapter 3, you may have already worked through this step. However, if you have uncovered new pain—and other people who precipitated it—you will want to go back to that chapter and walk through those steps with this person or persons in mind.

Almost always people who have been scarred by sexual abuse need professional counseling. Ask God to lead you to the right person if you need help.

Building a Relationship That Lasts

Sex should only be associated with a relationship that is lasting, and without marriage you are not committed to anything lasting, only to lasting as long as it feels good.

When Dr. Paul Meier consults with patients, he talks about the three-dimensional love between a husband and a wife: *agape*-love, *phileo*-love, and *eros*. God intends married couples to experience all these dimensions of love.

The *agape*-love is God's own unconditional love. *Phileo*-love is family love, the self-sacrificing love of strong family ties. And *eros*-love is romantic love, the passionate love that bonds two people together in an experience of emotional and physical fusion. "Another perspective on these three dimensions of love," Dr. Meier says, "is to view them as the (1) spiritual plane of love (*agape*); (2) the emotional plane of love (*phileo*); and (3) the physical plane of love (*eros*). In a Christian marriage, all three of these forms of love are intended to work together in harmony to produce a healthy, joyful, satisfying relationship."

Dr. Meier says that "when all three dimensions of love are fully functional in a marriage, both the wife and the husband are more open and receptive to the spirit of God."[5]

Then the circle of love is complete: God the Father, the husband, and the wife united in a circle of three, a loving relationship for life.

Scriptures to Consider As You Say No to Sexual Immorality

Look up theses scriptural passages and write the verses in the spaces below:

Matthew 5:32

1 Corinthians 5:1

1 Corinthians 6:13

Hebrews 10:26

Scriptures to Consider As You Walk Through a Season of Recovery from Sexual Abuse

Scripture can help you walk through a season of recovery from sexual abuse or sexual sin. Look up the passages and write the verses in the spaces below.

Scriptures to Encourage You
   Romans 8:1–2

   1 John 3:19–22

   Hebrews 10:19–22

What encouragement do these verses above offer the Christian adult who struggles with guilt resulting from victimization?

Scriptures to Give You Hope
   Joshua 1:5

   Hebrews 13:5

What message of hope do these verses offer to the Christian victim who feels abandoned?

Renounce the Occult

During my second counseling session with Mary Anne, she said, "I want you to renounce all your occult involvement."

My occult involvement? What's the big deal about that? I thought. It never entered my mind that dabbling with the supernatural was anything worth confessing. I had started slowly in the occult with Ouija boards, horoscopes, numerology, and transcendental meditation. Then I went full speed into astral projection, séances to summon the dead, hypnotism, Science of the Mind, and various Eastern religions.

Every occult practice I tried brought me an immediate high, but soon it was followed by a major letdown. None of it offered enough substance to sustain me for very long.

Mary Anne answered my questions about her request to renounce all occult involvement by reading the following Scripture:

> There shall not be found among you anyone who . . . practices witchcraft, or a soothsayer, or one who interprets omens, or a sorcerer, or one who conjures spells, or a medium, or a spiritist, or one who calls up the dead. For all who do these things are an abomination to the LORD. (Deut. 18:10–12)

"You not only need to stop practicing these things," she continued, "but you must renounce them before God and break the power of the satanic spirits behind them so they have no hold over your life."

How about you? Check the statements below that apply to you:

_____ "I have played with Ouija boards."

_____ "I have consulted the horoscope in the newspaper."

_____ "I have used numerology to predict the future."

_____ "I have had my fortune told."

_____ "I am fascinated with horror movies and go to every one possible."

_____ "I have played with tarot cards."

_____ "I have enjoyed music that glorifies evil."

_____ "I have practiced transcendental meditation."

_____ "I have been involved in witchcraft."

_____ "I have practiced hypnotism."

_____ "I have been involved in Eastern religions."

_____ "I have played ungodly computer games."

_____ "I have been learning about or involved in ESP (extrasensory perception)."

_____ "I collect satanic paraphernalia."

_____ "I have been a part of a séance."

_____ "I have been involved with telepathy, astral projection, or parapsychology."

You may think that reading your horoscope is harmless, but you're being deceived. It's not harmless; it's destructive.

Let's look at a biblical example of someone who bought into these occult practices: King Saul.

Saul began well. When the prophet Samuel anointed him as the first king of Israel, Saul was so humble he didn't consider himself worthy to be king. Right after that, he prophesied under the power of God's Spirit (1 Sam. 10:10). As king he won battles against the Philistines, one of Israel's toughest enemies, and the Ammonites. He refused to take vengeance upon those who questioned his anointing and authority as king (1 Sam. 11:12–13). Saul also ordered that mediums and witchcraft be removed from the land. In fact, because of Saul's leadership, all Israel reaffirmed its covenant with God (1 Sam. 11:14–15).

But unfortunately Saul began to stray. He did not always obey God's commands. He acted like a priest and made a sacrifice to God instead of waiting for Samuel to do it. He allowed the soldiers to keep some of the goods from the Amalekites' camp after Israel had defeated them—although God had told him to destroy everything. Each of these sins allowed the devil to take more and more of a hold on Saul's life. Eventually Saul became so jealous of David that he went into rages and repeatedly attempted to kill David.

At the end of Saul's reign, when the sight of a huge Philistine army advancing against Israel overwhelmed him, Saul turned to the occult. He consulted the medium of Endor to learn the outcome of the battle.

Are you tempted to turn to the horoscope or a fortune-teller when life's difficulties overwhelm you? Or when God does not answer your prayers or appeals? God didn't answer Saul's prayers to know the outcome of the battle with the Philistines because Saul had not followed God's previous directions. If you haven't walked with God or fulfilled the responsibility He has given you, you can't expect Him to give you further guidance.

Make sure you don't make the same mistake Saul made. He removed the sin of witchcraft from the land, but he did not remove it from his heart. You may denounce your association with the occult practices you checked above, but if your heart doesn't change, the sin will return.

How does God respond to Saul's disobedience? Scripture tells us: "So Saul died for his unfaithfulness which he had committed against the LORD, because he did not keep the word of the LORD, and also because he consulted a medium for guidance" (1 Chron. 10:13).

I have found that each experience with the occult will contribute to your depression, fear, and confusion. Believe me, I've been there. Occult practices don't work. But the danger is not that they don't work. The danger is that they work just enough to make you think they *do* work, and they suck you in. The danger is that the power behind them is real and intends to destroy you. Even though you may be just playing around, the devil isn't.

What the Bible says about the occult is clear. If we are aligned with it, we cannot be aligned with God. Pastor Jack Hayford says, "The occult is real in its power but wrong in its source. It derives its power from the realm of darkness." On the subject of astrology he says, "The danger of astrology is beyond a simple, superstitious misuse of time. Paying the trade of occult practices is to traffic with the demonic. It isn't the result of some cosmic influence radiating from the stars but a hellish one emanating from Satan himself, who has found but one more way to steal, to kill, and to destroy." We will take a more careful look at Satan and his accomplices in Chapter 12.

If you are involved in the occult now or have had any occult involvement, you must renounce it all before God. You can't be aligned with Satan and expect God to set you free. Jesus made this very clear when He said, "If a kingdom is divided against itself, that kingdom cannot stand. And if a house is divided against itself, that house cannot stand" (Mark 3:24–25).

Write a prayer in the space below. Confess any involvement with spirits other than the spirit of God. Mention them by name. Renounce them as satanic and bind the powers of darkness behind them—in Jesus' name. Then ask God to help you stay away from any satanic involvement in the future.

If you have been heavily involved in the occult, ask a pastor, a counselor, or another strong believer to pray for you to be set free from the bondage that accompanied it.

The day I renounced all my occult involvement and Mary Anne prayed for me to be set free, I felt a distinct sensation like an electrical charge pulsing through my head, throat, chest, stomach, and even my hands. Immediately I felt as if I had been released from a vise I had not even realized was there. I felt renewed strength, and I had a sense of peace, security, and well-being I had never known before.

Scriptures to Consider As You Are Renouncing the Influences of the Occult

Look up the Scriptures below to learn God's warnings about the influences of the occult. Write the verses that are most significant to you in the spaces following the Scripture passages.

Deuteronomy 18:9–14

Isaiah 8:19

1 Chronicles 10:13–14

CLEAN OUT YOUR HOUSE

After I had renounced the occult, Mary Anne instructed me to spend as much time as possible reading the Word of God in order to fill any empty space in me with the Lord's truth. I was eager to do that, so I decided to read straight through the Bible.

I hadn't read more than a few minutes about the rewards of obedience in Deuteronomy when I came across this verse: "Do not bring a detestable thing into your house or you, like it, will be set apart for destruction" (7:26 NIV).

Detestable thing? In my house? I wondered. *Do I have that, Lord? Show me if I do.*

Almost before the words were out of my mouth, I thought of my sixty or seventy books on the occult, spiritism, and Eastern religions. I had stopped reading them when I received Jesus and renounced my involvement in the occult, but I still had the books.

Now I knew what had to be done. I gathered twenty to thirty shopping bags and went to my bookshelves, a woman with a mission. I looked through each of my hundreds of books and discarded the ones about the occult or with any questionable material in them.

I didn't stop there, however. The more I thought about it, the more I recognized other offensive possessions. My search-and-destroy mission soon included paintings, sculptures, wall hangings, hand-painted trays, and miscellaneous artifacts that exalted other gods. I threw out records and tapes that were negative, satanic, or questionable in any way.

By then I felt so good that I thought, *Why stop there?* I threw out all my clothes that did not glorify God. Low-cut dresses, see-through blouses, and too-tight jeans were quickly discarded. I also gave away all reminders of my first marriage and old boyfriends and unhappy times.

How about you? Take an inventory of your possessions by checking the list below:

____ gifts from a former boyfriend or girlfriend if you are now married

____ things that remind you of people, incidents, or things that are not of the Lord

____ movies, books, or magazines that are sexually explicit

____ items that make you react negatively with depression, anger, anxiety, or fear

____ pornographic material

____ clothes that are revealing and not glorifying to God

____ paraphernalia with which to do ungodly things

____ paintings, pictures, or sculptures that involve Eastern gods or the occult

Now vow as David did in Psalm 101: "I will set nothing wicked before my eyes" (v. 3).

How about your children? When my son Christopher was young and having repeated nightmares, I prayed about him and felt led to go into his room and check his computer games. He had many, but I felt directed to pick up one that a Christian friend had loaned him for the week. There was nothing suspicious in any way on the outside, but when I checked the instructions, I found the worst satanic garbage.

With this in mind, take an inventory of your children's possessions. Bad things can come into your home via other people.

You won't enjoy the peace and quality of life you desire until you clean your house thoroughly. Replace whatever you take out of your life with something of the Lord. I bought Christian books and music to replace what I threw out. I searched for God-glorifying art and clothing.

Scripture says, "Let us purify ourselves from everything that contaminates body and spirit, perfecting holiness out of reverence for God" (2 Cor. 7:1 NIV).

This kind of purification has its roots in the Old Testament. After the occult reign of King Ahaz, Hezekiah brought the nation of Israel back to God. And one of the things this new king did was to "clean house." He removed the pagan altars, he cut down the wooden images, and he even broke in pieces the bronze serpent that had led the children of Israel through the desert (2 Kings 18:3–4). Unfortunately, the Israelites had begun worshiping this bronze serpent as if it were a god.

Hezekiah also cleaned God's house, which had been polluted during Ahaz's reign. He ordered the priests to destroy the "debris" and restored the articles that Ahaz had cast aside during his reign (2 Chron. 29:16–19). Hezekiah instituted a revival in the land that brought his people back to God. And that's what you are doing when you clean your house.

Since the time I originally went through my house carefully, I do this type of housecleaning periodically—never to the extent of this first experience, because I'm careful not to accumulate anything "detestable." But walking with the Lord fine-tunes our discernment, and things I've never seen as harmful before are now revealed as promoting destruction. I have also dedicated each home I've lived in to the Lord.

A Spiritual Dedication

It's also a good idea to pray over your home to clean it out spiritually. Every time we've moved to a different house, we've asked a small group of believers to come over and help us pray through it. We walk the boundaries of the property and every room, praying for the peace and protection of God to reign supreme there.

If you have never prayed over your house, apartment, or room, do it immediately. If you can, join with one or more believers to pray and ask for these things:

• that God's peace and protection will be over your home;

- that nothing evil can enter it; and

- that any point of bondage finding a place there will be broken.

The less contact you have with what is not of God, the more of God you can have in your life, and the more you will know His love, peace, joy, healing, and wholeness.

Scriptures to Consider
As You Clean Out Your Home

Look up the Scripture passages below as you clean out your home. Write the verses that are most significant to you in the spaces below the Scriptures.

2 Chronicles 29:15–19

2 Kings 18:3–6

Proverbs 3:33

Psalm 101:2–4

9

Take Care of Your Body

*D*uring my teens and early twenties, intense negative emotions provoked one stress-related disease after another in my physical body. I had everything from problem skin, headaches, and chronic fatigue to infections and allergies. Several months before I received the Lord, I had become so weakened that I developed sores in my mouth and could barely eat or talk. The doctor I went to for help said that I had a severe vitamin B deficiency. He plunged a needle into my right hip and emptied a large syringe of vitamin B, which hurt so badly I could hardly stand up.

However, ten minutes down the freeway, I started to feel like a new person. And by the time I pulled into my driveway, I experienced a strange and amazing sensation of hope.

I took the doctor's advice and over the next few days went back to a routine of proper eating and exercise.

We can't have good emotional health without a certain amount of physical health. In fact, we can suffer from depression or some other negative emotion simply because of physical depletion or imbalance. If I feel discouraged, depressed, overwhelmed, or fearful, I check first to see if I have been taking proper care of my physical health. Right alongside the steps you are taking toward emotional wholeness, you must be taking steps toward physical wholeness.

First of all, you should have regular checkups to make sure you are in good health. Then you need to be aware of seven important factors, which I presented in my book *Greater Health God's Way;* these factors must be in balance to achieve consistently good health.

Seven Factors to Achieve Consistently Good Health

1. Ask God to show you the stress in your life.

Stress is the response of your mind, emotions, and body to whatever demands are being made upon you.

Take an inventory of your present emotional health by checking the statements below that apply to you:

_____ "I feel rejected because _____."

_____ "I am angry at _____."

_____ "I always feel lonely."

_____ "I am afraid of _____. Sometimes this fear cripples me."

_____ "I often feel anxious."

_____ "I can't help feeling sad much of the time."

If you are experiencing any of the emotions listed above, your body is carrying a load it wasn't designed to carry. The effect of stress on your body is not so much what happens to you as how you respond to it.

Look at the factors you identified above. List them below and then note in the proper column what you can do to respond to them.

Emotion	Change the Situation	Learn to Live with It
1.		
2.		
3.		
4.		

5.

6.

Sometimes stress is so hidden, we don't realize we're being affected by it. The important thing to remember is that the ultimate reaction to stress is death. That's why we must learn to recognize stress in our lives before it gets serious and then take specific steps to alleviate it.

2. *Ask God to show you the truth about the food you are eating.*

Are you eating too many impure or processed foods that are depleted of essential vitamins and minerals?

Take an inventory of your eating habits by checking the statements below that apply to you:

_____ "I eat too much candy, cake, and ice cream."

_____ "I eat too many fried foods."

_____ "I drink too many soft drinks."

_____ "I don't drink very much water."

_____ "I frequently skip breakfast and sometimes other meals too."

_____ "I eat highly processed foods containing chemicals."

_____ "I don't worry about eating a balanced diet."

_____ "I eat very few vegetables or fruits."

If you checked any of these statements, you are making it difficult for your body to repair and cleanse itself. Toxic wastes can pile up in your body, causing physical stress that interferes with the body's functions. When you don't feed your body properly, you become physically depleted, your mind cannot process information accurately, and every decision is exhausting. What we eat can also determine how we react to situations in our lives.

In Dr. Kenneth Cooper's book *Regaining the Power of Youth at Any Age*, he suggests that people "eat at least five to seven servings of fruits and vegetables—including at least one helping of 'cruciferous' vegetables—every day."[1] Cruciferous vegetables (so named because their flowers grow in the form of an X-shaped Greek cross)—broccoli, brussels sprouts, cauliflower, and cabbage—reduce the risks of cancer, heart disease, and constipation.

Some women also may need to look more carefully into their eating habits, because they may be suffering from an eating disorder, like anorexia or bulimia.

How about you? Take another inventory of your eating habits by checking the statements below that apply to you:

_____ "People tell me I am too thin, but I don't believe them."

_____ "I think about food all the time."

_____ "I sometimes go on eating binges during which I eat large amounts of food, so much that I feel sick and make myself vomit."

_____ "I use laxatives to help me control my weight."

_____ "My family quizzes me about what I eat."

_____ "I get upset when people push me to eat more."

_____ "I find myself panicking for fear of gaining weight if I cannot exercise."

_____ "Lately I'm more depressed and irritable than usual."

_____ "I fear gaining weight or becoming fat."

If you checked more than four of these statements, you might be suffering from an eating disorder. Seek help from a Christian counselor immediately. Your changing metabolism and out-of-control hormones will cloud any progress you make toward emotional restoration. Making food a ritual, a religion, or the center of your life causes it to become your enemy.

3. Ask God to show you about exercise.

The main purpose of exercise is to keep the body healthy by enabling it to do four extremely important functions: eliminate poisons, increase circulation, strengthen muscles, and eliminate stress.

I believe that everyone needs to exercise, regardless of age, size, or shape. What will differ among individuals will be the type of exercise that appeals to them and suits their lifestyle. You can choose from the following: an aerobics class, dance class, bicycle riding, swimming, jogging, fast walking, handball, or even horseback riding. People are always surprised when I mention horseback riding. They think the horse is doing all the exercising. Not so. You're using practically every muscle in your body to keep good balance and control—and you're stimulating your bones, organs, and muscles.

I often suggest that people try walking as a family affair or think of physical activity as a social event. Bicycle around the block with your child or grandchild. Take a hike in the mountains with a friend. Walk in the evenings with a family member.

4. Ask God to show you about drinking water.

Water is involved in every single process in our bodies, including digestion, circulation, absorption, and elimination. It is a primary transporter of nutrients through the body, and it carries poisons out of the body.

Think about this:

- People so often drink fluids other than water that thirst is no longer an adequate indicator of the body's need for water.

- Not having enough water can cause exhaustion, memory loss, and the inability to focus.

- Most people don't drink enough water.

For these reasons, and many more, we should make sure we drink about eight eight-ounce glasses of water a day. Use a filtering system or buy bottled water from a reputable company. Although it is best to drink the entire amount as water, you can also add a little fruit juice to it for flavor, which will make it easier to drink.

Dr. Cooper quotes the researchers at the Nutrition Information Center, who say that a good rule of thumb is to assume that for every cup of coffee or other dehydrating beverage you drink (such as tea or sodas that are not decaffeinated), you should add an extra cup of water. Dehydrating drinks cause the drinker to urinate more frequently, thus losing fluids from the body.[2]

5. Ask God to show you about prayer and fasting.

Fasting with prayer is an important spiritual step, which I will explain later. This is also important for your body as a natural self-healing and cleansing process. During a fast the energy ordinarily used to digest, assimilate, and metabolize is spent purifying the body.

6. Ask God to show you about spending time daily in fresh air and natural sunlight.

Natural light is a powerful healer, germ killer, remedial agent, and relaxer. Scientists are now discovering that light has a significant effect on the immune system and the emotions. Any activity or exercise done outside increases your inhalation of fresh air, which also aids in cleansing the body of impurities. Of course, you need to use the appropriate sunscreen to protect your skin and you need to be balanced. Don't bake but don't lock yourself in a dark hole either.

7. Ask God to show you about getting enough rest.

You need to be able to achieve a deep, sound, completely refreshing sleep naturally, without drugs. During sleep, food is transformed into tissue, the entire system is cleansed of poisons, and the body repairs itself and recuperates. Those things can only happen fully during sleep when the nervous system slows down. Sleeping pills, alcohol, or drugs interfere with those processes.

If everything is working properly in your life, good sleep comes automatically. If it doesn't, it usually means that one or more of the other six areas of health care is out of order.

How about you? Are you getting enough sleep? Check the statements below that apply to you:

_____ "I am irritable a lot of the time."

_____ "I feel tired most of the day."

_____ "I have headaches fairly often."

_____ "I am having difficulty concentrating."

_____ "I am feeling depressed and anxious."

If you checked a couple of these statements, you might be suffering from some sleep deprivation. Dr. Kenneth Cooper gives several remedies for this problem.

Avoid alcohol, caffeine, and smoking. Dr. Cooper says that these three substances work against a good sleep. Avoid them, especially just before bedtime.

Establish a firm hour for bedtime. Try to maintain a consistent hour for bedtime. Discipline yourself to go to bed then, Cooper recommends.

Break your "worry loops." Cooper suggests that you pick a poem or Bible verse and begin to repeat it silently after you turn out the light. If you find your mind wandering, turn back to the words you've chosen. Cooper says that most likely, you will never make it past twenty or thirty repetitions before you're sound asleep.[3]

Try not to view taking care of your health as an overwhelming and complex task. It's really not. It's the way God wants us to live, and it's a point of obedience. Ask Him to help you.

In the days ahead you might want to repeat this Scripture to yourself, inserting your name in the blanks, as you vow to take care of your body:

"Therefore, whether you, _____, eat or drink, or whatever you, _____, do, do all to the glory of God." (1 Cor. 10:31)

Scriptures to Consider As You Work to Take Care of Your Body

Look up these Scriptures and write them in the spaces below.

1 Corinthians 3:16–17

1 Corinthians 6:19–20

1 Corinthians 9:27

1 Corinthians 10:31

Romans 12:1

WATCH WHAT YOU SAY TO YOURSELF

*T*here's been a lot of talk in recent years about what parents, teachers, and other adults have done to children when they are young. Some of that has centered around the words they have spoken to these little folk. All of us, even small children, carry on a conversation with ourselves—within our minds and sometimes aloud. It's a dialogue that plays over and over again in our minds—and one that can be both good and bad, just like the words of parents, teachers, and other adults.

Throughout my first thirty years I spoke many negatives to myself—"I'm a failure" . . . "I'm ugly" . . . "Nothing ever goes right for me"—until one day the Holy Spirit spoke to my heart through Proverbs: "Death and life are in the power of the tongue" (18:21). A quick inventory of the things I had said aloud and in my mind revealed that I had been speaking death. This thought was frightening.

Yet when we constantly speak negatively about ourselves or our circumstances, we cut off the possibility of things being any different than what we've just spoken.

How about you? Is your internal dialogue positive or negative? Check the statements below that correspond to your own thoughts:

_____ "There's no way I can do that. I'm just not capable."

_____ "Nobody really cares about me."

_____ "I'm a failure."

_____ "I'm ugly."

_____ "Nothing ever goes right for me."

Unfortunately, we often take what we hear the devil saying to our minds and think it's truth: "You're such a failure. You'd be better off dead." Or we repeat to ourselves what someone else said to us years ago: "You're worthless." The Bible says, "You are snared by the words of your mouth" (Prov. 6:2). That includes our silent messages to ourselves as well as what we speak aloud. We need to ask ourselves, "Who is speaking to us? Is it the voice of God, is it our flesh, or is it the devil?"

Let's take the statements above and test these negative thoughts against God's Word to us in Scripture.

"There's no way I can do that. I'm just not capable."

God promises, "Fear not, for I am with you; / Be not dismayed, for I am your God. / I will strengthen you, / Yes, I will help you, / I will uphold you with My righteous right hand" (Isa. 41:10).

We can't have a more positive statement than that. The holy God of the universe will help us with His right hand.

"Nobody really cares about me."

The apostle Peter, who walked with the living Christ, advised the early Christians to cast "all your care upon Him, for He cares for you" (1 Peter 5:7).

Each of us has someone who cares for us: our Heavenly Father. We can't do any better than that.

"I'm a failure."

Scripture says, "He who has begun a good work in you will complete it until the day of Jesus Christ" (Phil. 1:6).

No Christian is a failure. God has begun a good work in us, which He will fulfill. He's guiding the ship of our lives, we are the cooperating crew—and that ship is on a successful mission!

"I'm ugly."

The psalms say that we are "fearfully and wonderfully made" (Ps. 139:14). The verse says that God's works are "marvelous." How can any one of us be ugly?

Genesis 1:27 and Ephesians 2:10 also say that we are made in the image of God. Remember that when you feel ugly or awkward. Say to yourself every day, "I am fearfully and wonderfully made. God says so!"

"Nothing ever goes right."

The apostle Paul advised the Galatians, who probably felt much this same way, "And let us not grow weary while doing good, for in due season we shall reap if we do not lose heart" (Gal. 6:9).

None of us can see the end of our activities when they seem to be floundering; only God knows what's being accomplished, and He promises "all things work together for good to those who love God" (Rom. 8:28).

When talking to yourself about yourself, always speak words of hope, health, encouragement, life, and purpose. We all have a choice. We can replace negative thoughts with positive ones, like:

- "I am a child of God. I have value."
- "The Lord will help me do what's right. That's all that matters."
- "God will enable me to get the job done, one task at a time."

Take a moment now and write a positive internal dialogue for yourself, like the ones above:

This is God's truth to you. I'm not suggesting that you lie to yourself. Be honest about your feelings.

If you are feeling discouraged, admit it. But also bring God's truth into the situation. Rather than saying, "Life is the pits," say, "I feel sad today, but I know God is in charge of my life and will perfect all that concerns me" (paraphrase of Ps. 138:8). If you can't think of anything positive, say, "Lord, show me Your truth about me and my situation."

Write a prayer below, asking God to help you confront negative thoughts with positive ones:

Don't allow negative speech to work against what God wants to do in you. And don't be hard on yourself. Treat yourself with respect and kindness. Say, as David did, "I have resolved that my mouth will not sin" (Ps. 17:3 NIV).

Scriptures to Consider As You Watch What You Say to Yourself

Write the passages of Scripture in the blank spaces and then summarize what each Scripture means to you.

Jeremiah 31:3

Romans 8:28–29

Philippians 4:13

Revelation 21:7

Ephesians 2:10

FAST AND PRAY

At our first counseling session, Mary Anne suggested that I fast for three full days, drinking only water, before our next meeting. I did as she said, drinking water and praying every time I felt hungry. After the first day, the hunger pangs weren't that bad.

But when she called to cancel our appointment and reschedule it for the following week, I had to fast three days again. Through that second week I became discouraged and my depression returned. The fasting was hard and I wanted to give up, but I obeyed anyway. On the day of my counseling appointment, I prayed for a miracle, but I was really afraid to hope for one.

Yet the morning after the appointment, I woke up without depression. Day after day I waited for it to come back, but it didn't. I believe that fasting helped me to be set free with greater speed and completeness.

Why Fast?

God designed fasting to bring us into a deeper knowledge of Him, to release the Holy Spirit's work in our lives, and to bring us to greater health and wholeness. In fact, the Bible says certain spirits can only be broken through fasting. When Jesus' disciples asked why evil spirits didn't submit to them, He replied, "This kind can come out by nothing but prayer and fasting" (Mark 9:29).

Fasting is like getting a holy oiling so the devil can't hold on to you. It's designed "to loose the bonds of wickedness, to undo the heavy burdens" (Isa. 58:6).

Who doesn't need the power of God to penetrate her life and circumstances? So what's holding us back? Ignorance and fear. We are ignorant of what the Bible says on the subject, and of what fasting can accomplish, and of all of its wonderful benefits. We are afraid of the hunger, headache, nausea, weakness, and dizziness that can accompany infrequent fasts.

Yet there are more than eighty references to fasting in the Old and New Testaments. Jesus Himself fasted for forty days and forty nights in the wilderness.

Fasting is a spiritual exercise and discipline during which you give yourself completely to prayer and close communion with God. It's a time to sensitize your soul to His Spirit and to see Him work mightily on your behalf.

How Should I Fast?

Once you are convinced of the rightness of fasting, you need to take the first step. Begin by simply skipping a meal, drinking water, and praying at the time you would ordinarily eat. Say, "God I fast this meal to your glory and to the breaking down of strongholds in my life." Then lift up in prayer all the areas where you know you need freedom. Say, for example, "Lord, I fast this day for breaking down strongholds the devil has erected in my mind through depression, confusion, unforgiveness, or anger."

The next time, try skipping two meals. Then see if you can work up to a full twenty-four- to thirty-six-hour water fast once a week. I fast about forty days a year, but I do it one day a week for forty weeks. I actually look forward to it as a time to hear God more clearly.

If you have a physical limitation and cannot water fast, then go on a vegetable or fruit fast, denying yourself everything but vegetables or fruits for a day. My book *Greater Health God's Way* has a chapter on fasting to help you move into that discipline.

In Isaiah 58 God gives guidelines for fasting by examining the Israelites' current practices. The people were fasting, all right, but they were not "walking the walk"; their actions did not show any follow-through. God says if your fasting is going to please Him you should:

- Stop oppressing those who work for you. Treat them fairly (v. 6).

- Share your food with the hungry and welcome wanderers into your home (v. 7).

- Keep the Sabbath day holy (v. 13).

In other words, walk your talk!

I recommend that you read the entire chapter of Isaiah 58 each time you fast to remind yourself of exactly why you are fasting (to be free), what you are to do (give of yourself), and what your rewards are (healing, answered prayer, deliverance, and protection).

The Lord gives an additional guideline for fasting in Matthew: do so in private, He says (6:16). And almost everywhere fasting is mentioned in Scripture, prayer accompanies the discipline. Fasting can only be effective if it humbles us before God and brings closer communication with Him.

Be sure to accompany your fast with prayer. Fasting without prayer is just starvation. This is a time to be close to the Lord and to allow Him to guide you where you need to go. Sometimes you will have the clear leading of the Holy Spirit as to why you are fasting; sometimes you won't. Whether you do or not, it's good to have a prayer focus in mind.

Remember that "no discipline seems pleasant at the time, but painful. Later on, however, it produces a harvest of righteousness and peace for those who have been trained by it" (Heb. 12:11 NIV).

Write a prayer below, asking God to speak to you about fasting. And if it is His will that you fast, ask Him to help you do so physically and under the guidelines He has suggested:

Because fasting is an instrument for defeating the enemy, it's a key to deliverance and emotional wholeness. Don't neglect it. Even after you have been set free, Satan will be looking for ways to put you back into bondage. Be determined to slip through his fingers by walking in this step of obedience.

Scriptures to Read As You Consider Fasting

Look up the passages below, note the verses that are significant to you, and answer the questions. What do these passages tell you about fasting?

Psalm 35:11–13

Why did David fast?

What was the result of his fast?

Psalm 69:5–10

Why did David fast here?

Daniel 9

Why did Daniel fast?

Step 3
Find Deliverance

Recognize who your enemy is and separate yourself from anything that separates you from God or keeps you from becoming all He made you to be.

DELIVERANCE? WHAT'S THAT?

When Mary Anne told me I needed deliverance that day in the counseling office, her words resounded in my head. Immediately I thought of red-eyed demons, green vomit, and whirlwinds. *Am I possessed?* I wondered.

When I questioned Mary Anne about this, she explained, "I'm talking about *oppression* and *not* possession. There are spirits that attach themselves to you. They can come into anyone's life through the work of the devil, who has been allowed influence and access through our own sin."

"Will I become a different person?" I asked.

"Deliverance doesn't *change* you into a different person. It *releases* you to be who you really are," she explained.

Still I wondered, *If I need deliverance from demonic bondage, am I really saved?*

Pastor Jack Hayford answered the question when he spoke to the church the following Wednesday evening. "You can't get any more saved or forgiven than you are when you come under the covenant of the blood of the cross of Jesus. Deliverance has to do with possessing the full dimensions of what Christ has for us. It has nothing to do with being demon-possessed, or being destined for hell, but it has to do with being rid of residual fragments of hell from your past. Residue from the past often manipulates us. Deliverance sets us free from that."

In the next days I realized that I desired deliverance more than I feared it. And in the coming months I was set free of depression, fear, torment, unforgiveness, bitterness, and a lifetime of other bondage as well. I know firsthand that Jesus is the Deliverer and that deliverance is real and available to anyone who seeks it.

Possession or Oppression?

You are body, soul, and spirit. Your spirit is the very core of your being. Your body is the outer layer. In between those two is the soul, which is made up of your mind (what you think), your emotions (what you feel), and your will (what you decide to do). Satan can oppress your mind and emotions, influence your will, and attack your body, but if you've been born again, he *cannot* touch your spirit. If you are filled with the Holy Spirit, you absolutely cannot be demon-possessed. *The American Heritage Dictionary* defines the word *possession* as "the state of being dominated by or as if by evil spirits."[1]

When you were born again, your spirit was covered by the blood of Jesus. Satan can't touch your spirit because "He who is in you is greater than he who is in the world" (1 John 4:4). *Jesus* is in you. Evil spirits *are not* in you. However, Satan can touch your soul, and you *can* be demon *oppressed.*

The American Heritage Dictionary defines the word *oppression* as "something that oppresses or burdens, a feeling of being heavily weighed down, either mentally or physically."[2]

Note the difference. Possession is complete domination. Oppression is a burden, the feeling of being heavily weighed down. The torment of oppression can be very real and miserable, and God wants to release your soul from any demonic oppression.

The Devil?

Some of you may think, as I once did, that the devil is just a myth. If so, you need to look around you. Who entices men to sexually assault children? Who causes men to become serial killers? Why is there evil in the world?

Christian singer Steve Camp will tell you that Satan is alive and well and active in the world. He tells of an encounter with the cult Satan's Choice in *soul 2 soul*, written by Christopher L. Coppernoll.

Steve Camp heard that Satan's Choice had been allowed to hold meetings at a certain university in Canada—but Christians were prohibited from doing so. Camp prayed and acted and received permission to hold the first Christian music concert at this school during his next Canadian tour.

As the crew was preparing for the concert that day, some local satanists called the stagehands and threatened, "If this Christian singer, Steve Camp, sings about Jesus tonight, we're going to kill him."

When Camp arrived at the auditorium, someone told him that the head of the satanic coven was on the phone and wanted to talk to him.

The man told Camp there were fifty members in his coven and then reiterated the threat: "If you sing about Jesus tonight and preach the gospel, we're going to hurt you."

Camp replied with scriptural truth. He quoted Philippians 1:21—"For to me, to live is Christ, and to die is gain."

"You mean you're not afraid of our god?" the man asked.

"What god?" Camp replied. "Satan is not God! He's a created being, a fallen angel, walking around with a crushed head—doesn't sound like much of a god to me." Then Camp invited the coven to be his guests at the concert that night.

And they did attend. As Steve Camp was sharing the gospel, these men and women threw things at him on stage and shouted in an "interesting form of the Greek language."

Camp asked them to sit down and be quiet; he would talk to them after the concert, he assured them. They did not stop heckling. Finally Camp said, "In the name of Jesus Christ, sit down."

And they all sat down. (His motto from that time to now is: "Walk softly and carry a big Bible!")[3]

Okay, you say, so many people believe Satan is real—but who is he?

Who is the devil?

The church does not spend a great deal of time characterizing Satan since Scripture tells us to keep our eyes on Jesus, not the devil. However, we need to know who our enemy is so that we can recognize his attacks— and defeat him.

I have listed several important Scriptures, which will give you a clear picture of Lucifer. Write the passages in the spaces and then note what that tells you about Satan.

1. Revelation 12:7–10

Satan was _____. Now he roams _____.

2. Isaiah 14:12–15

Satan's sin was _____. His goal was _____.

3. 1 Peter 5:8

Satan is _____. His goal now is _____.

You must be aware of two facts about the prince of darkness:

- Satan is not all-knowing and is not able to be more than one place at a time. His power is limited by God. Read the first two chapters of the book of Job and watch as Satan has to ask God's permission to test Job.

- In the end Jesus will triumph over Satan, who will be cast into the lake of fire and brimstone.

But Satan does have power until the end of this world. And he has an army of demons who also disobey God and do the devil's will. Let's look at what we know about them.

Who are the devil's accomplices?

Again I ask that you do a Bible study so you can truly understand your adversaries. Write the Scripture verses in the following spaces and then note what the verse tells you about Satan's accomplices, the demons:

1. Revelation 12:7–9

Who was cast out of heaven with Satan? _____. Is it not probable that these entities are still aligned with Satan as his demons?

2. Luke 8:26–31

The demons were _____. They were able to _____.

Yet God does not leave us stranded when the devil or his demons threaten us. He has overcome the powers of darkness—and He gives us the power to withstand the devil. Jesus gives us the authority to resist demons, just as He did His disciples: "Behold, I give you the authority to trample on serpents and scorpions, and over all the power of the enemy, and nothing shall by any means hurt you" (Luke 10:19).

Each of us is responsible for our lives. Spirits can only possess what is given to them. God does not overrule human will. *And you don't have to choose the will of hell for it to happen; it will happen if you are not actively choosing the will of God.*

How Can a Person Be Demon Oppressed?

In my book *Lord, I Want to Be Whole,* I give seven reasons for demon oppression. To decide if you might be under demonic oppression check any statements below that might apply to you:

_____ "I have been in direct disobedience to God's laws."

_____ "I have nursed some long-term negative emotions."

_____ "I have been involved in an occult practice." (This includes reading your horoscope in the paper or playing with a Ouija Board.)

_____ "I experienced a time of great tragedy or trauma, and I have never been able to get over the grip of grief."

_____ "I was extremely hurt when my _____ (father, husband, mother, friend) did _____. I have never been able to forgive this person."

_____ "I have given up on God." Or "I have blamed God for something that happened." (This is a hardening of your heart against God.)

_____ "My _____ was an alcoholic (or an adulterer or had a violent temper) and I tend to be the same way too." (This is called the multigenerational chain of dependency: "visiting the iniquity of the fathers on the children to the third and fourth generation," Num. 14:18.)

Did you check any of the statements above? If so, you could be oppressed because you have directly disobeyed God's laws, or carried long-term negative emotions, or practiced the occult, or been disillusioned after the death of a loved one or a time of great disappointment. Or you could have hardened your heart against God or inherited spiritual bondage. Any of these situations can give the devil a hook into your life. You may need deliverance.

Nothing to Fear

Don't let the word *deliverance* frighten you or put you off. It's not scary or strange. Deliverance is the severing of anything that holds you, other than God. It could be a spirit of fear, of anger, of lying, of depression, or of lust. It could be a behavior you've acquired for self-defense, like compulsive over-eating or a habitual withdrawal from people. Being born again delivers us from death, but we need to be delivered from the dead places in our lives as well.

The real question is, have you allowed an evil spirit to express itself through you by sinning? Are there any places in your life where a power other than God's is in control?

To determine this let's look at James, chapters 3 and 4. In these chapters James, the brother of Jesus and a leader in the Jerusalem church, identifies the sins the devil uses to gain a stronghold in our lives. James 4 is one of the most complete chapters in Scripture on spiritual warfare, but his discussion of spiritual warfare begins in chapter three.

The Sins of Relationship

In chapter 3 James focuses on sins of relationship, which result, he says, from evil "wisdom." The first sin mentioned is a sin of the tongue, "a little member" that "boasts great things" (v. 5). And in chapter 4 James cautions, "Do not speak evil of one another, brethren" (v.11).

Have you committed sins of the tongue? Gossiping? Lying? Cursing? If so, list those sins below and the circumstances in which they were committed:

Then James goes on to talk about another relationship sin: bitterness.

Do you have bitterness in your heart? Go through the inventory below:

Bitterness against others (mention who and why):

Bitterness against your circumstances (mention what and why):

Bitterness against yourself (mention why):

Bitterness against God (mention what and why):

But James is not finished with relationship sins yet. Two others are prominent in this chapter: self-seeking and boasting. Are you guilty of any of these sins? If so, list those sins below and the circumstances in which they were committed.

Self-seeking (pursuing one's own interest above everyone else's):

Boasting:

James tells us that these prideful attitudes open the door to "confusion and *every evil thing*" (3:16, emphasis added). That's certainly a good reason for admitting them and then confessing and repenting.

If you do so, James promises that you will receive wisdom from above, which "is first pure, then peaceable, gentle, willing to yield, full of mercy and good fruits, without partiality and without hypocrisy" (3:17).

Stop a moment now to write a prayer, asking for God's forgiveness for any of the sins you identified. Tell Him that you will turn your back on these sins in the future—and ask His help to do so.

But James still isn't finished with the list of sins that give Satan a stronghold in our lives. He completes that list in chapter 4: fighting, lust, murder, and adultery.

Have you committed any of these sins? If so, list them below.

If you have, James says, "Do you not know that friendship with the world is enmity with God? Whoever therefore wants to be a friend of the world makes himself an enemy of God" (James 4:4).

However this enmity between you and God is not permanent—if you repent. James makes this clear. He says, "But He [God] gives more grace. Therefore He says: God resists the proud, / But gives grace to the humble" (4:6).

Write a prayer below, asking God to forgive you for these last sins. Again, tell Him that you will turn your back on these sins—and ask His help to do so.

Now tear these pages out of your workbook. Your sins are forgiven. The devil's sway is broken. James says, "Resist the devil and he will flee from you" (4:7).

And James promises, "Draw near to God and He will draw near to you . . . Humble yourselves in the sight of the Lord, and He will lift you up" (4:8,10).

No matter what kind of bondage you suffer, ask God to show you where you need deliverance. Then ask Jesus, the Deliverer, to deliver you and to show you what you must do. You don't need to become preoccupied with the demon or the bondage; you need only to seek the Deliverer. He'll take care of the rest.

Seven Basic Steps to Deliverance

No matter when, where, or how deliverance occurs, seven steps are common. Ignoring them may short-circuit the flow of deliverance in your life.

1. Confessing

You have already worked through the inventory of your sins. And you have confessed them to God. If you are still struggling, James suggests this: "Confess your trespasses to one another, and pray for one another, that you may be healed" (5:16). But you must be careful about this. A Christian pastor, a Christian counselor, or a mature Christian within your church would be a credible person. You might even establish an accountability situation with a mature Christian. But beware of someone who is not mature and might repeat your confession to others.

2. Renouncing

Confessing is speaking the whole truth about your sin. Renouncing is taking a firm stand against that sin and removing its right to remain in your life.

The first step in renouncing sin is to ask God exactly what you need to be delivered from. If you're dealing with evil spirits, ask Him to show you which ones.

You may have identified these spirits as you worked through the sin inventory in this chapter. If not, take a moment now to look back at this inventory so you can identify the spirit that might be behind this sin. Is the spirit one of fear? If so, cast it out. Choose a Scripture that applies to your own life. For example, say, "God has not given [me] a spirit of fear, but of power and of love and of a sound mind" (2 Tim. 1:7).

Write a prayer below renouncing any spirit that might have control of your life. Be sure to address the spirit directly. Then say, "You have no power over me. I bind you in the name of Jesus Christ and in the authority He has given me." Finally, ask God to protect you from that spirit in the future.

3. Forgiving

If one of the sins you identified in your inventory was a response to the actions of another person and you haven't forgiven that person, do so now. Write that person's name below:

Now write a prayer, telling God that you have forgiven this person.

If you still feel unable to forgive this person or persons, go back to chapter 3 and work through the steps of forgiveness mentioned there. And remember: do not use this person to escape the reality of your own sin. We are responsible for what we do, regardless of what has happened to us.

4. Speaking

When we have been delivered from anything, our joyful proclamation cements in our minds what God has done in our souls. The Bible says, "Let the redeemed of the LORD say so, / Whom He has redeemed from the hand of the enemy" (Ps. 107:2). This keeps the enemy from trying to steal away what God has done. Say, "Jesus has delivered me from this, and I refuse to give place to it any more."

You might also want to be truthful about your sin to help someone else cope with the same problem. Alcoholics Anonymous has adopted this approach, in which sponsors have helped thousands of alcoholics recover from their addiction. At the end of his epistle James says, "Brethren, if anyone among you wanders from the truth, and someone turns him back, let him know that he who turns a sinner from the error of his way will save a soul from death and cover a multitude of sins" (James 5:19–20).

Is God calling you to speak out about the deliverance He has given you? Pray about this and listen for His reply.

5. Praying

In the first part of chapter 5, James gives further instruction about spiritual warfare. He says, "Is anyone among you suffering? Let him pray" (v. 13). And later he says, "The effective, fervent prayer of a righteous man avails much" (v. 16).

James goes on to give an example of answered prayer. He reminds the early Christians that Elijah was a man, just like us. He prayed that God would create a drought to show His power over the god Baal, who was supposed to bring rains and bountiful harvests. *And it did not rain in Gilead for three years and six months.* And then Elijah prayed again, this time asking for the drought to cease, *and the rain poured down* (1 Kings 17:1, 18:1).

We have this same power through prayer.

How is your prayer life? Do you pray every day? If not, commit to doing so in the future. Ask God to help you. Deliverance happens by praying to God from the depth of your being. It can be one or more believers praying together with you, or just you alone simply crying in the presence of the Lord. Psalm 34:17 says, "The righteous cry out, and the LORD hears, / And delivers them out of all their troubles."

6. Praising

After James advises anyone who is suffering to pray, he asks another question, "Is anyone cheerful?" If so, he says, "Let him sing psalms" (5:13).

Worship invites God's presence, and in the presence of God deliverance happens.

7. *Walking*

James works the early Christians through an inventory of their sins at the beginning of chapter 4, and then he declares, "Therefore submit to God" (v. 7). This is the only way to live the Christian life. James describes the attitude of such a faithful walk at the end of the chapter: "Come now," he says, "you who say, 'Today or tomorrow we will go to such and such a city, spend a year there, buy and sell, and make a profit'; whereas you do not know what will happen tomorrow. For what is your life? It is even a vapor that appears for a little time and then vanishes away. Instead you ought to say, 'If the Lord wills, we shall live and do this or that'" (James 4:13–15).

To see how important submission is to your everyday walk, work through the Scripture verses at the end of this chapter. Then write the most significant passage on an index card to carry in your purse. Every time you see this card, remember that you have submitted every part of your life— your marriage, your children, your work, your desires—to Jesus.

Once you have taken these seven steps you still need to be continually on guard. In his book *What You Need to Know about Spiritual Warfare*, Max Anders says, "Spiritual conflict takes two forms: temptation and spiritual opposition. When we are tempted to sin, we are to flee (2 Tim. 2:22). When we are confronted with spiritual opposition, we are to fight (James 4:7).

"Most of us, however, have a genius for reversing the two. When we sense spiritual opposition in our life and ministry, we want to flee. And when presented with temptation to sin, we want to stand and fight. That is contrary to the Word, and we will have little success until we get it straight."

Anders gives several examples to illustrate his point. For instance, "Do you want to run away from your financial obligations? Stand and fight. Is it too hard to improve family relationships? Stand and fight."

But "Are you tempted to toy with a relationship that isn't Christ centered? Flee. Are you tempted to put together a deal that isn't totally honest? Flee."[4]

Deliverance, then, is evicting the devil and refusing to be crippled by him. Each morning say, "Lord, fill me afresh with Your Holy Spirit this day and crowd out anything that is not of You."

If we maintain our submission to God, if we remember to fight when there is spiritual opposition and to flee when we are tempted to sin, we overcome much of our tendency to sin. After all, God is in control.

Remember that Steve Camp concert in Canada? The one where the Satan's Choice members harassed him—and threatened to kill him?

According to the ticket count, forty-five satanists attended the concert that night. And at the end of the invitation, thirty out of those forty-five satanists received Jesus Christ as their Lord and Savior![5]

God will win in your life. Calvary insures that.

Scriptures to Consider As You Submit Your Life to the Lord

Read the Scriptures below and note the verses that are most important to you. Surrendering to the Lord is the key principle to victory in spiritual warfare.

Ephesians 1:22–23

Philippians 2:9–16

Colossians 2:9–10

1 Peter 3:18–22

Romans 12:1–2

1 Corinthians 6:19–20

Step 4

Seek Total Restoration

Refuse to accept less than all God has for you and
remember that finding wholeness is an ongoing process.

13

THE PATH TO RESTORATION

As I've mentioned, my definition of emotional health is having total peace about who you are, what you're doing, and where you're going, both individually and in relationship to those around you. Unfortunately, John Trent could never find this peace in his relationship with his father. Therefore his path to restoration was not complete.

John's parents were divorced when he was three months old. Although his father always lived a few miles away, John didn't see his dad until his teenage years. At that time his dad promised to watch John and his twin brother, Jeff, play one of their high-school football games.

For the first time, their dad would watch them play sports. The boys were elated—and played their hearts out that game. But Dad wasn't there, after all. He'd gotten sidetracked at work.

And John's dad wasn't there for father-and-son banquets or for John's birthday or for Christmases or other holidays. Throughout his life, John Trent searched for his dad's blessing.

One day in 1991 John sat beside his dad as he was waking up after heart surgery. When his dad awoke they talked briefly before John had to leave.

"I love you, Dad," John said as he got up to go.

"I love you, too, John."

John couldn't believe what he had heard. "What did you say?"

"I love you, too, John."

The next day John asked his dad if he would call John's two brothers and tell them that he loved them, as he had told John the night before.

His father not only refused to make the call, he denied he'd ever said those words to John. "It must have been the drugs they have me on!" he joked. But John wasn't laughing. He was back in the same quagmire he'd lived in all his life: searching for a parental blessing that constantly eluded him. He did not have peace in his relationship with his father, and his total restoration was blocked.[1]

Because our restoration is often ongoing and done in layers, total deliverance doesn't happen overnight. God is the only one who knows which layer should come off first and when it should happen.

My first major deliverance (from depression) came in a counseling office after three days of fasting and prayer. My next experience with major deliverance (from child abuse) happened over a period of time as I sought the presence of God. I found deliverance from a spirit of fear as I took simple steps of obedience. I was delivered from self-sufficiency as I sat in church listening to the teaching of God's Word on grace. I experienced deliverance from a hardness of heart as I worshiped God with other believers in church. I received deliverance from emotional torment as I cried out to God in my prayer closet alone in the middle of the night. Layer after layer of bondage has been stripped away, with no two instances identical.

I've learned not even to try to second-guess God. His ways are far above ours, and He is much too creative for our limited minds to comprehend His thoughts and actions. Even though we glimpse His ways in times spent in His presence, we can never predict how He will accomplish deliverance next. The only thing we can know for sure is that as long as we want Him to, He will continue to work deliverance in us until we go to be with Him.

There are times after you've been delivered from a particular thing that the same old problem seems to be coming back. You may feel as depressed and emotionally hurt as you ever did, if not worse, and you'll fear you're going backward. But if you've been walking with the Lord and obeying Him to the best of your ability, then you can trust that God is wanting to bring you to a deeper level of deliverance than ever before. This process may feel just as painful, if not more so, but the new level of freedom will be far greater than you've experienced before.

God knows when you're ready for the next step. It may not be exactly the way you want it at the moment, but there is always deliverance available to us anytime we make ourselves available to it. We must sustain a spirit of grateful dependence upon Him and be willing to say as David did, "You are my God. / My times are in Your hand; / Deliver me from the hand of my enemies" (Ps. 31:14–15).

A year after surgery, John Trent's dad died of his heart problems. One morning John returned from jogging to see his seven-year-old daughter, Kari, crying.

"What's the matter, Honey?" he asked as he held her in his arms.

"It's Grandpa," she said. "He's gone now . . . and I never got to hug him."

John describes that moment this way: "I can't tell you how much that 'unguarded moment' cut my heart. I had Scriptures memorized to remind me of my wholeness in Christ (Col. 2:10). I had God's Word that I was His child, and a much loved son (Heb. 12:7; John 3:16). I knew that He would never leave me or forsake me (Heb. 13:5). Yet I also discovered that I wasn't quick enough to out-logic an emotion.

"All the hurt, all the pain, all the memories of empty arms, and even more painfully empty arms for my children, spilled out. Both Kari and I cried in the hallway. We grieved his loss all over again."[2]

Being born again doesn't remove you from emotional conflict, spiritual oppression, or satanic attack. And being delivered once doesn't mean you never need deliverance again. In fact, the devil will keep trying to gain back a point of control in your life. You can count on that.

Is It Possible to Find Deliverance Without a Counselor?

God would not be so unfair as to say, "There is deliverance for you, but you must find yourself a good deliverance counselor in order to get free." He has provided a way to be free by seeking the presence of Jesus, the Deliverer. Whether you are isolated on an island, lost in the woods, or sentenced to solitary confinement, Jesus is there if you seek His presence and cry out to Him for deliverance. "Where the Spirit of the Lord is, there is liberty" (2 Cor. 3:17); and "from the LORD comes deliverance" (Ps. 3:8 NIV).

Finding deliverance by being in the Lord's presence does not mean seeking His presence for five minutes and then doing your own thing. It means remaining in His presence all the time. It means deciding you will walk in the spirit and not in the flesh.

Walking in the spirit means saying with conviction, "I don't want what the devil wants; I want what God wants." It means facing the hell in your life and knowing every part of you wants nothing to do with it because "those who live according to the flesh set their minds on the things of the flesh, but those who live according to the Spirit, the things of the Spirit" (Rom. 8:5).

John Trent never received the blessing from his dad; as an alcoholic, John's father was unable to give a blessing. Yet all of us are able to walk through these steps by ourselves, to reparent ourselves.

Have You Received the Blessing?

In their book *The Gift of the Blessing*, John Trent and Gary Smalley give the following definition of a family blessing: "A family blessing begins with *meaningful touching*. It continues with *a spoken message* of *high value*, a message that pictures *a special future* for the individual being blessed, and one that is based on *an active commitment* to see the blessing come to pass."[3]

They say that children who haven't received the blessing often come from specific types of families. Check the statements below to see if you came from one of those families:

_____ "I never felt that my parents loved me. They seemed to prefer my sister (brother)."

_____ "My parents smothered me with affection and seemed to withhold it from my sibling(s)." If you checked this statement, you come from a home where there was a flood and a drought of the blessing: one child was drowned by his or her parents' love, the other never received it.

_____ "Nothing I accomplished ever seemed to quite measure up to my parents' expectations." If you checked this statement, you come from a home where the blessing was just out of reach.

_____ "I felt that my parents attached strings to their love. I had to do everything they asked to receive it." If you checked this statement, you come from a home where the blessing was exchanged for a burden.

_____ "I was expected to be a _____. My career was predetermined for me." If you checked this statement, you come from a home where there were unyielding family traditions.

_____ "My parents were divorced (or my mother/father left home when I was young). I never received my _____'s blessing because I never saw him/her on a regular basis." If you checked this statement, you only received a part of the blessing. Your parents may have been divorced, as John Trent's were, or one of your parents may have deserted the family.

Checking any of the previous statements means that you may be longing for approval from a parent. You have never received a family blessing. And this may be keeping you from receiving total restoration.

But you can give yourself that blessing by taking the five steps that Smalley and Trent suggest for a parent in their best-selling book.

Give Yourself the Blessing

1. Meaningful Touch

A parent's hugs and kisses bless a child. When Isaac blessed his son Jacob, he embraced him and kissed him, even though Jacob was forty years old at the time. And then Jacob (whose name was changed to Israel) passed on this blessing to his grandchildren, Joseph's sons:

Joseph said to his father, "They are my sons, whom God has given me in this place." And he said, "Please bring them to me, and I will bless them" . . . Then Joseph brought them near him, and he kissed them and embraced them . . . Then Israel stretched out his right hand and laid it on Ephraim's head. (Gen. 48:9–10,14)

If you didn't receive the blessing, have a mature Christian lay hands on your head and pray a blessing over you.

2. Spoken Words

"Abraham spoke a blessing to Isaac. Isaac spoke it to his son Jacob. Jacob spoke it to each of his twelve sons and to two of his grandchildren," Smalley and Trent remind us.[4]

Write the words below that you wish your mom or dad had said to you (like "I'm really proud of you" or "You are really special"):

Then speak these words to yourself or have that Christian friend pray them over you.

3. Expressing High Value and Picturing a Special Future

We will look at these two steps of the blessing together because they can be interlinked.

Smalley and Trent say that to "value something means to attach great importance to it." This, they say, is at the very heart of the concept of blessing. "This is what the patriarchs in the Old Testament did in blessing their children. . . . Isaac pictured his son as someone that other people, including his own family, should greatly respect. He was even someone who deserved to be 'bowed down to' by nations because he was valuable."[5]

Picturing a special future can be an outgrowth of expressing high value. "You have a special gift for math; therefore you could become a highly respected engineer."

If you have never had a parent express your value to you, write down how you would like to be valued in the space below. For instance, "You have always been such a caring person; you will be a wonderful mother."

Write words like these in the space below and circle them, highlight them, star them so you won't ever forget them.

Now offer these thoughts to the Lord. Say, "God, this is how I would like to be valued."

4. An Active Commitment

Smalley and Trent suggest that parents make an active commitment to take three steps as their children grow up: commit the child to being blessed to the Lord, commit their lives to the child's best interests, and become a student of those they wish to bless.[6]

I suggest that you make a commitment to do this for yourself. Feel God's blessing when you read this paraphrase of the blessing in Numbers 6:24–26 aloud:

> The LORD bless me and keep me;
> The LORD make His face shine upon me,
> And be gracious to me;
> The LORD lift up His countenance upon me,
> And give me peace.

Then commit to becoming attuned to what is important to your own well-being. That can be something as simple as eight hours of sleep each day or as involved as taking a class in an area of your giftedness.

Finally, study your abilities. Become a student of yourself by answering the questions below and thinking about them in the next week.

What are you particularly good at? List three things in the space below. (And don't think, "I'm not good at anything." That's Satan talking, not your heavenly Father. He created you in His image and has a high purpose for your life.)

1.

2.

3.

Now, how should that influence your future? Set some goals in the space below:

Write a prayer in the space below, asking God to help you continue your deliverance with the guidance of His Holy Spirit.

If you do all these things and are still having problems in a specific area, don't hesitate to seek professional Christian counseling.

Counselors for His People

A counselor who has discernment and revelation from God can identify the source of your problem and give you the truth of God that will set you free: "Where there is no counsel, the people fall; / But in the multitude of counselors there is safety" (Prov. 11:14).

This is not only a case for counseling but also for seeing more than one counselor in your lifetime. God wants you to seek *His* counselors because He wants you to know *His* counsel. Psalm 1:1 says, "Blessed is the man / Who walks not in the counsel of the ungodly." Your counselor must be lined up with God's Word and God's laws.

The Holy Spirit is the greatest psychiatrist you will ever find. Jesus said, "And I will ask the Father, and he will give you another Counselor to be with you forever—the Spirit of truth" (John 14:16-17 NIV). Spiritual problems will not subside until they are addressed in the spirit realm. Only counselors who know *the* Counselor can help you do that.

Unfortunately, counseling used to carry a stigma. "That's just for the mentally ill, the emotionally weak, people who are 'messed up,'" some said.

Not so. Counseling is for anyone who is caught in the stressful, complex web of human interaction called life, anyone who wants to grow into a new level of completeness. Most of us can use some wise counsel at one time or another. Be released in the knowledge that seeking good Christian counseling is not only beneficial but biblically right. Proverbs 19:20–21 tells us:

> Listen to counsel and receive instruction,
> That you may be wise in your latter days,
> There are many plans in a man's heart,
> Nevertheless the LORD's counsel—that will stand.

How to Select a Counselor

Even Christian counselors need to be qualified and highly recommended. Consider the following questions as you look for a counselor:

- Does my church have a counseling service or a recommended list of counselors?

- Is the counselor a Christian?

- Do I know a mature Christian who has received good counseling from this person?

- What are this counselor's credentials?

And then be sensitive to the Holy Spirit as you meet with the counselor in the first session.

As You Walk Through Counseling

Always weigh what the counselor says against the Word of God; if it holds up, then follow his or her instructions. If you are asked to attend church regularly, read the Bible an hour a day, and stop seeing that married man, then do those things. Hearing His counsel and refusing to abide by it is a serious offense. The Bible describes people who wouldn't listen to God's counsel as:

> Those who sat in darkness and in the shadow of death,
> Bound in affliction and irons—
> Because they rebelled against the words of God,
> And despised the counsel of the Most High. (Ps. 107:10–12)

However, if your counselor recommends actions that violate God's Word, then you have the wrong person. Leave him or her immediately and keep searching for the right one.

Write a prayer below, asking God to help you and your counselor uncover the areas of deliverance in your life. Ask Him to help you to not be discouraged if this takes longer than you wish. Finally, commit to walking step by step with Him so that you can become all He created you to be:

John Trent ultimately did receive a blessing. His grandfather gave him what his father never did. After his parents' divorce, his grandparents came to live with the three boys and their mom. John's granddad was "a wonderful man, but a stern disciplinarian. He had rules for everything— and swats to go along with all his rules!" And one rule was: "Be home before the street light comes on!"

One night John and his twin brother didn't make the curfew. And John earned two swats from grandpa—and his blessing.

His grandmother told John to get his grandfather for dinner. When John looked in his grandpa's room, he saw something that shocked him: "a man who rarely showed any emotion was sitting on the end of the bed, crying."

Suddenly his grandfather saw him. John froze where he was. He hoped catching grandpa crying wasn't a sixty-swat offense.

Instead of a spanking, his grandfather said, "Come here, John." Then he reached out and hugged John. "John, I want more than anything in life for you and your brothers to grow up to become godly young men. I hope you know how much I love you, and how proud I am of you."

Grandpa was crying because he regretted having to punish John!

John Trent says, "I can't explain it, but when I left his room that night, I was a different person because of his blessing . . . For years afterwards, recalling that clear picture of my grandfather's blessing helped to shape my attitudes and actions."[7]

God blessed John through his grandfather.

We can do all we know in order to be set free, but we must remember that it is the Lord who will accomplish it. Just be sure that you continue to look to Him for total restoration. And don't give up.

Finding Total Restoration

Look up the Scripture passages below and note the promises of restoration that are most meaningful to you.

Jeremiah 30:17

Psalm 23

Psalm 118:5–9

2 Corinthians 1:9–10

Galatians 6:1

Step 5

Receive God's Gifts

Acknowledge the gifts God has given you
and take the steps necessary to receive them.

God's Gifts of Love and Grace

*I*magine someone giving you a present wrapped in shiny paper with an exquisite bow on top. You say, "Thank you so much for the gift. The paper is beautiful, the bow is breathtaking, and I will cherish it forever." Then you put the gift on the table and let it sit unopened. How sad for the giver who had spent time, effort, and resources to give this gift to you.

Often our heavenly Father gives us gifts, and we don't unwrap them or possess all He has for us because we don't see them or we don't realize they are there for us.

God gave us two monumental gifts: the gift of His Son, Jesus (John 4:10), and the gift of His Holy Spirit (Acts 2:38). From those two gifts all His other gifts flow. Gifts such as righteousness (Rom. 5:17), eternal life (Rom. 6:23), prophecy (1 Cor. 13:2), and peace (John 14:27) are just a few of the many good things God gives us.

Of the countless gifts God has for us, four are crucial to your emotional healing, restoration, and continued wholeness: the gift of His love, the gift of His grace, the gift of His power, and the gift of His rest. We will look at two of these gifts—His love and His grace—in this chapter, and the other two in the next chapter.

Unfortunately some of us, like Lori Graham Bakker, haven't felt God's love through the love of our earthly fathers.

Receive God's Gift of Love

Lori's handsome, six-foot dad was a strict disciplinarian who rarely interacted with his three children. Her two brothers—Mark and Scott—and

Lori often joked about their dad's imaginary List. Whichever of his three children was in his good graces at the moment was at the top of the List. But that ranking changed from day to day, from month to month, and from year to year. And one of the kids was always off the List. Bob Graham was a very controlling person who played the children against each other.

In her book, *More Than I Could Ever Ask*, Lori Graham Bakker says, "What I wanted was the one thing he couldn't give me: his unconditional love. I never once felt that I could crawl up on his lap uninvited. I just wanted him to love on me, just wanted him to say he was proud of me."[1]

What little bond existed between Lori and her father began to be severed when she was only eight years old. One evening when her mom was attending night classes at Arizona State University, Lori accidentally overheard her dad's phone conversation. "I love you, too, doll face," he was saying. "And I want to see you soon."[2]

Lori didn't understand adultery at that age, but she knew something was wrong at their house. When she was twelve, her best friend's older sister confirmed her fears. The girl worked part-time in the shoe department with Lori's dad, and she'd heard him talk to his girlfriends on the phone, just as Lori had when she was eight. This proof of her father's affairs changed Lori's life.

Food helps us grow physically and education helps us grow mentally; in the same way, it takes love for us to grow emotionally. If we aren't nurtured with love, our emotions stay immature, and we are always searching for the love we never had. Unfortunately some of us yearn so much for love that we look for it in all the wrong places. That's what Lori Graham Bakker did.

After she found out about her father's affairs, she began hanging out with the wrong crowd, smoking pot, and looking to boys for the love she didn't get from her dad. At the age of seventeen she fell in love with Jesse, a handsome twenty-six year old who moved in across the street.

Their relationship began with marijuana and quickly evolved into sexual promiscuity. When Jesse asked her to marry him, she agreed although she knew that he was mainlining drugs and had been frequenting topless bars. The day before they were married, a drunk Jesse attacked Lori, claiming she had been with another man.

Yet she still married Jesse the next day. Lori was hungry for love—and she didn't know any way to satisfy that hunger. But in the spirit, there is another way: receiving the love of God.

God's Love Shows No Favoritism

After I received Jesus, I could sense the strong presence of God's love, and I had no trouble believing that He loved everyone. Everyone else, that is. I had a hard time believing that He loved me. It took some time of walking with Him (learning about His nature, allowing Him time to answer my prayers, seeing that His Word was truth, and receiving His deliverance) before God's love really sank into my being.

If you think God couldn't love you because you're not worth loving, you need to understand that He loves differently from us. Lori Graham found this out, but not until she was thirty-one years old.

One Easter Sunday she decided to go to Phoenix First Assembly of God Church. She smoked a joint as she got dressed for the sunrise service. After the service, she stayed for a Sunday school class where Pastor Jack Wallace was preaching on forgiving others who had wronged you. Just the night before, her ex-husband, Jesse, who had beaten her during their ten-year marriage, had called asking her to lend him one thousand dollars. They'd been divorced for four years, yet he was expecting her to bail him out of jail.

Sitting in Jack Wallace's Sunday school class several hours later, the wounds from her marriage were still fresh and raw. Yet the pastor was saying, "You must make a conscious choice to forgive that person so you can go on with your life." Then he began to speak about God's forgiveness for sin, and how Jesus Christ paid the penalty for our sins. You can receive divine forgiveness, he said, by receiving Jesus into your heart.

Lori made a conscious choice to forgive Jesse; she knew it was necessary for her own survival. Then she prayed for salvation right there in her chair, asking Jesus to come into her heart, to cleanse her from her sin, and to give her a new life.

Just before noon that day she walked down the long aisle of the main sanctuary and knelt at the altar as she repeated the Sinner's Prayer. Finally she felt God's love and forgiveness.

As Lori Graham learned, you can do nothing to make God love you more—and nothing to make Him love you less. The Bible says, "The same Lord over all is rich to *all* who call upon Him" (Rom. 10:12, emphasis added). He loves you as much as He loves me or anyone else.

Believing Is Receiving

The key to receiving God's love is deciding to believe that it is there for you and choosing to open up to it. The Bible says, "The LORD's unfailing love surrounds the man who trusts in Him" (Ps. 32:10 NIV). Nothing can separate us from God's love except our own inability to receive it. Hear God speaking directly to you by writing your name in the following Scripture:

Yes, I have loved you, _____, with an everlasting love;
Therefore with lovingkindness I have drawn you, _____.
(Jer. 31:3)

Write a prayer in the space below, asking God to help you feel this kind of love today, tomorrow, next year, and for the rest of your life.

Then say, "God, I trust Your love for me and all that You say in Your Word about me and my circumstances." The more you say this over and over during the day, the more you will experience God's love in your heart.

My prayer for you is the same prayer that the apostle Paul prayed for the members of the early church:

I pray that Christ will be more and more at home in your hearts as you trust in him. May your roots go down deep into the soil of God's miraculous love. And may you have the power to understand, as all God's people should, how wide, how long, how high, and how deep his love really is. May you experience the love of Christ, though it is so great you will never fully understand it. Then you will be filled with the fullness of life and power that comes from God. (Eph. 3:17–19 NLT)

My prayer for you is that you will experience this depth of God's love for yourself in the days ahead. I've found that God's love is always more than we expect. That's why we are brought to tears so often in His presence. They are tears of gratitude for love beyond our imagination.

Receive God's Gift of Grace

Not As We Deserve

I spent fifteen years learning to understand what was accomplished on the cross, and it simply means that Jesus took all that I have coming to me—pain, sickness, failure, confusion, hatred, rejection, and death—and gave me all that He had coming to Him—all wholeness, healing, love, acceptance, peace, joy, and life. Because of God's grace, all we have to do is say, "Jesus, come live in me and be Lord over my life."

In my early twenties my lifestyle was motivated by a desperate need for love. Among the disastrous by-products of this lifestyle were two abortions in less than two years. Both were ugly, frightening, and physically and emotionally traumatic (not to mention illegal at the time), yet I felt relief more than remorse about them. Only after I began to walk with the Lord and learn of His ways did I see what I had done.

When Michael and I decided to have a baby, month after month went by and I didn't get pregnant. I, who had gotten pregnant so easily before, thought surely I was being punished for my abortions.

"God, I know I don't deserve to give birth to new life after twice destroying life within me," I prayed. "I deserve to be childless. But please have mercy and help me to conceive."

He answered that prayer, and my two children—Christopher and Amanda—have been the greatest example of God's mercy and grace to me. The Lord even sent me an adopted son, John, to mother after his own mom and dad died. *God gave me exactly what I did not deserve.*

Grace has to do with it all being *Him. He* does it. Not us. Grace is always a surprise. You think it's not going to happen, and it does. Pastor

Jack Hayford teaches this about grace: "When the humble say, 'I don't have it and I can't get it on my own,' God says, 'I've got it and I'm going to give it to you.' That's God's grace."

The difficult part of receiving God's grace is maintaining a balance between thinking *I can do whatever I feel like doing because God's grace will cover it all,* and believing *Everything in my life—my success, my marriage, how my kids turn out, how whole I become—depends totally on what I do.* Neither extreme exemplifies grace and mercy, but people who have been emotionally damaged often fall into the latter category.

Feel God's grace for you today, regardless of what you have done, by inserting your name in the Scripture below:

My grace is sufficient for you, _____, for My strength is made perfect in weakness. (2 Cor. 12:9)

End this chapter by writing a prayer below, asking God to help you feel His grace from this day forward.

Scriptures to Remember As You Seek to
Feel God's Love and Grace

The Bible tells us that God freely gives His love and grace to us. Write the passages in the spaces below and feel God's assurance that you will always have His love and grace.

God's Gift of Love

John 14:23

John 3:16

God's Gift of Grace

2 Corinthians 12:9

Ephesians 2:4–10

1 Timothy 1:12–16

2 Corinthians 9:8

GOD'S GIFTS OF POWER AND REST

*I*n this chapter we will look at the two other gifts God has given us: His gift of power and His gift of rest—and how we can receive those gifts.

God's Gift of Power

God's power is a gift for us to use, among other things, for the healing of our souls, and anyone wanting emotional health and restoration must have access to it. God wants you to know the "exceeding greatness of His power toward us who believe" (Eph. 1:19), so He can "strengthen you with power through his Spirit in your inner being" (Eph. 3:16 NIV).

To receive His power you first have to receive Him and know who He is. You also have to know who your enemy is and be convinced that God's power is greater. Hear God speaking to you through the Scripture as you insert your name in the blank space:

> He who is in you, _____, is greater than he who is in the world (1 John 4:4).

With that knowledge, look for the power of the kingdom in your life.

The Keys of the Kingdom

Pastor Jack described the keys of the kingdom as being similar to the keys to his car. "There is very little power in the key that fits my car," he explained, "but that engine with all its power does not come to life without my key being put into the ignition. I don't have the power to go outside and get myself going sixty miles an hour, but I have access to a resource that can get me going that speed.

"Jesus said, 'I will give you the keys of the kingdom of God.' Keys mean the authority, the privilege, the access. Some things will not be turned on unless *you* turn them on. Some things will not be turned loose unless *you* turn them loose. Some things will not be set free unless *you* set them free. The key doesn't make the power of the engine, it releases the power of the engine."

Pastor Jack made the distinction that the kingdom of God means the realm of His rule. Our will must be submitted to His until we are completely dependent upon His power. As Pastor Jack says, "His keys don't fit our private kingdom. His power is unleashed upon command, but not for our own personal gain."

God promises to give you His power. Remember Jesus' words to His disciples, which are also for us. Hear Him speaking directly to you as you insert your name in the blanks:

> I give you, _____, the authority to trample on serpents and scorpions, and over all the power of the enemy, and nothing shall by any means hurt you, _____. (Luke 10:19)

Because human nature inevitably works itself back into bondage, we are always in need of a fresh flow of the Holy Spirit. Ask for one daily. Every morning say, "God, I need a fresh flow of Your Holy Spirit power working in me. I am weak, but You are all-powerful. Be strong in me this day."

What good are God's keys to you if you never use them to unlock any doors to life? What good is God's power if you never receive and use it? Open the gift of power He has given you. Your life depends on it.

God's Gift of Rest

In August of 1999 Lori Graham Bakker went to visit her dad in Phoenix. She knew his diabetes was poisoning his body and wanted to spend some time with him. One day, as she was driving him to the drugstore for his medications, he grew quiet, then said, "I want to ask your forgiveness for something, Lori Beth."

Lori was amazed. She couldn't ever remember her dad asking anyone for forgiveness.

"Remember that Christmas you wouldn't come see me because I was so mad at you? I was wrong about that."

Her dad had been furious because Lori had taken her niece, the daughter of her brother Mark, to the inner city to spend a part of Christmas day with a family Lori had adopted as part of her ministry there.

"It's okay," Lori said. "I forgave you a long time ago."

But her dad continued to apologize, asking her to forgive him for everything he had done to her—and for all the things he should have done but hadn't.

"I've forgiven you all along," Lori said. "All through the years. There were many times I was hurt, but I chose to forgive you."[1]

A couple of days after that, Lori's dad died. When she called her brother Mark to tell him, she told him about their dad asking for her forgiveness. "He even told me he was proud of me. . . . I waited all my life to hear those words."

Later that day she felt she should stop and praise God for her father. No matter how much he had hurt her, he was her dad, and she had loved him. "I want to thank You for Dad's life, as crazy as it was," she told her heavenly Father. "Even with all the pain, there were fun times, and I'm grateful for those."[2]

Peace filled her heart. She had found rest in her relationship with her father.

Resting in Him

Rest is "an anchor of the soul" (Heb. 6:19), which keeps us from being tossed around on the sea of circumstance. It's not just the feeling of ease we get from a sound sleep at night; true rest is a place inside ourselves where we can be still and know that He is God, no matter what appears to be happening around us.

Do you feel like David did in Psalm 55:4–6? He wrote:

> My heart is severely pained within me . . .
> Fearfulness and trembling have come upon me,
> And horror has overwhelmed me.
> So I said, "Oh, that I had wings like a dove!
> I would fly away and be at rest."

How many times have you felt that way? You feel pressed by anguish, trouble, pain, worry, and fear, and you feel that the only way to find rest is to escape. But God commands you to pray and deliberately take time to rest in Him.

Jesus says, "Come to Me, all you who labor and are heavy laden, and I will give you rest" (Matt. 11:28). He instructs us not to allow our hearts to be troubled but to decide to rest in Him. We must say, "God, I choose this day to enter into the rest You have for me. Show me how."

When we do that, God reveals all that stands in our way. Pray this prayer again and write down what stands in the way of your rest in the space below:

Now write a prayer in the space below, asking God to change you and your life so that nothing will keep you from the rest He has for you.

Finally, rest in Him. Resting is "casting all your care upon Him, for He cares for you" (1 Peter 5:7) and learning to be content no matter what the circumstances (Phil. 4:11). It's being able to say, "God is in charge, I have prayed about it, He knows my need, I am obeying to the best of my knowledge. I can rest."

God's gift is that we should have one full day of rest every week and not lose anything by doing so. This means rest for the soul as well as rest for the body—a day of vacation from our concerns, problems, deadlines, needs, obligations, and future decisions. It's spending time with Him because your "soul finds rest in God alone" (Ps. 62:1 NIV). If God Himself observed a day of rest in creating the world (Gen. 2:2–3), how can we expect to survive without it?

All of God's gifts are important. And He promises to give them to you: "If you then, being evil, know how to give good gifts to your children, how much more will your Father who is in heaven give good things to those who ask Him!" (Matt. 7:11).

Don't miss out on any of God's gifts in your life. After all, you want *everything* He has for you.

Scriptures to Remember When You Are Looking for God's Power

God's power is described frequently in the Old Testament, and His promise of power is prevalent through both the Old and New Testaments. Look up the passages below and note the verses that are most significant to you.

Descriptions of God's Power

Exodus 15:6–10

Psalm 59:16, David's experience of God's power

Promises That He Gives His Power to Us

Throughout the Bible God gives power to His people. The same power is available to us if we are walking with Him.

2 Samuel 22:32–34

2 Chronicles 25:8

Psalm 71:18

2 Corinthians 12:9

Scriptures to Remember When You Are Looking for God's Rest

Look up the passages below. In them you will see God establishing the Sabbath as a day of rest. You will also learn the reasons God sometimes withholds His rest. And finally you will read His promise of rest to Moses and to us. Note the verses that are significant to you.

God Establishes the Sabbath as a Day of Rest

Exodus 23:10–12

Exodus 31:15–17

Reasons God Withholds His Rest

Hebrews 3:7–11

Why does God withhold His rest in this passage?

Hebrews 4:3–7

Why does God withhold His rest in this passage?

Hebrews 4:3–7

Revelation 14:11

Why does God withhold His rest in this passage?

God's Promise of Rest to Moses—and to Us.

Exodus 33:14

Step 6

Reject the Pitfalls

Avoid or get free of the negative traps and
deceptions that rob you of life.

16

BEWARE OF THE PITFALLS

As a child I remember a day when my dad fell into a literal pitfall. At the time we lived on a small ranch in Wyoming. He was riding a horse on the prairie when he fell into a hidden crevice, which was about fourteen feet deep, much too deep for him to get out by himself. Time passed as he sat there helpless. His horse's legs were broken, and his own situation became more serious as the hours went by.

When we finally realized Dad was missing, my uncle went out to search for him. Thankfully he was able to find Dad in the unending prairie wilderness and get him out of that deep crevice. Unfortunately, the horse had to be shot and killed to relieve him of his pain.

I often compare that crevice to the pitfalls in our lives: they're hidden. We can be walking along and not see them. Yet they are deep traps—and they can be equally as dangerous as that Wyoming crevice. That's why we have to stay close to the Holy Spirit. God knows the way, and He will lead us away from these traps if we will follow Him and stay close to His word.

Unfortunately, we are all susceptible to being deceived in some way. Deception is Satan's plan for our lives. But here's the good news: *We don't have to listen to his lies.* Yet we do have to examine our thoughts in the light of God's Word to see if they line up properly, because the devil will use everything you don't know about God against you.

In Step Six I want to make you aware of sixteen of the most common deceptions. We can so easily be sucked into any of these that we don't even see it happening. Personally, I've been snared, or at least tempted at one time or another, by every one on the list. I hope this will help you identify the traps before you fall into them; or help you to combat them if you have, like me, already succumbed.

The Pitfall of Abortion

THE LIE: *"I have my rights. It's my body."*

*L*ori Graham Bakker's search for love led her to fall into the pitfall of abortion. Soon after she married Jesse, she became pregnant. But Jesse didn't want a child. "Maybe someday," he said, "but not right now."[1] Lori had always wanted to be a mom, but she decided that she could wait until she and Jesse had been married a while. She went to a Planned Parenthood clinic where she was assured that the five-minute abortion procedure was safer than having a baby.

I bought into a similar lie. "It's not a human being; it's just a mass of cells," I was told. Like Lori Graham Bakker, I was deceived, and I had little conscious guilt about taking the life of another person through abortion. But that didn't make it any less wrong or the consequences any less shattering.

Deception is walking, thinking, acting, or feeling in opposition to God's way and believing it's okay to do so. It's also believing that things are a certain way when they really aren't. Satan is the deceiver, and we are deceived when we line ourselves up with him.

Lori Bakker was told that the five-minute abortion procedure was completely safe. In the next four years she had four more abortions. For a year after her fifth abortion, in 1980, Lori experienced a great deal of pain in her right side. An ultrasound showed a grapefruit-sized cyst on her right ovary. The doctor said he might have to remove one ovary but assured Lori that she could still become pregnant.

But when the operation was performed, the surgeon was astonished. Lori's insides were mangled. There was a large amount of scar tissue and signs of a massive infection. The doctors felt they had to do a complete hysterectomy or Lori's life would be threatened.

"A five-minute procedure. Safer than having a baby." One of those "safe" five-minute procedures had destroyed Lori's ability to have children—and almost taken her life.

The deception of abortion is thinking that because it's legal, there is nothing wrong with it. But when the very existence of another person hangs in the balance, it can no longer be just a matter of *my* life, *my* rights, and *my* choice. There is someone else to consider, and not to recognize that is to be deceived indeed.

In my own particular situation, I was desperate at the time of my abortions. I attributed the ill feelings to my own embarrassment. When I became a Christian, I read Scripture that confirmed my questions. I read:

> Before I formed you in the womb I knew you;
> Before you were born I sanctified you. (Jer. 1:5)

> For You formed my inward parts;
> You covered me in my mother's womb. (Ps. 139:13)

Then I read medical accounts of babies surviving outside the womb as early as the fifth month of pregnancy. I had to admit that I'd destroyed someone God had created with abilities and gifts. I wept. No, I mourned.

Lori Graham Bakker also grieved. She had had five abortions by the age of twenty-one. She had been on the pill, but because of drug usage she sometimes forgot to take one or two pills.

If you have been deceived as I was, you might want to walk through the grieving process that Lori's friends Chris and Jolene, who had attended a post-abortion healing conference, led Lori through.

At the time Jolene told her, "If you'd had a stillborn child or even a miscarriage, friends would have consoled you, and you would have mourned. But women who've had abortions—women like us—actually had the same kind of loss, yet we never had the experience of grieving for our children."

Chris and Jolene began by anointing Lori with oil as they asked God to reveal whatever memories she had that needed to be healed. Blocking out memories of the event is a defense mechanism, which must be overcome so the suppressed pain can surface.

Do you have any memories of abortion? Note those memories below:

Then Lori's friends asked her to name each of the babies she had aborted. Lori said, "I don't know how I know this, and it probably sounds weird, but I think I know the sexes of my children." But she couldn't understand what her friends were asking her to do. "Name them? . . . But why?"

"Because they're your children, and they're in heaven now," Jolene said.[2]

Lori gave them all Bible names: Adam, Sarah, Joseph, Paul, and Hannah.

Once Lori had named the babies, Chris told her how important it was for her to forgive her ex-husband for wanting her to have the abortions. She also needed to forgive the doctors and nurses and the girlfriends who drove her to the clinic—everyone involved.

Are there any people you should forgive? If so, list them below:

As Lori Bakker did this, she realized that the number-one person she had to forgive was herself. She believed that God had forgiven her, but she still hadn't forgiven herself.

In August 1989, a few months after her salvation, Lori felt God's forgiveness for her abortions. She had been driving to the beach when she listened to Focus on the Family and heard a broadcast of "Tilly," the story of Kathy, a depressed woman who had a dream about lots of children without names or parents—but she didn't know where they came from.

Children in heaven with no names and no parents, Lori had thought. *A woman who is depressed and doesn't know what is wrong.* Lori knew what was wrong with this woman; Lori had been in her shoes. She too had had an abortion.

Later on the beach, Lori thought about her abortions. When she could bear these thoughts no longer, she felt the comforting presence of the Holy Spirit wrap around her like a soft cashmere shawl.

On the beach that day, Lori Graham realized that God had already forgiven her for the abortions, and she was finally able to forgive herself.

You might want to also add your name to the list of people you want to forgive. Then write a prayer in the space below, asking God to help you forgive the people you listed:

Now tear these pages out of this book and burn them. The slate is clean. You are forgiven and so are the others on that list.

After asking Lori to name her aborted children, Chris and Jolene gave her symbols of her babies: handkerchief dolls made of white linen. Lori held them and grieved as songs about abortion and children played in the background.

If you have had this kind of experience, you might want to picture your aborted babies and name them. Allow yourself to grieve for these children.

Or you might want to write a letter to the baby or babies in the space below:

Now commit the baby or babies into God's hands.

As Lori did this she felt an indescribable peace seep into her broken, empty soul. And on the heels of peace came a quiet joy—the kind of joy she never thought she would be allowed to have.

Lori Graham Bakker titled her book *More Than I Could Ever Ask* because God has given her more blessings than she could ever have imagined. He inspired her to start a ministry to women who've had abortions, called "Mourning to Joy." He led her to meet a man, Jim Bakker, the televangelist, who also had a past he regretted. Lori says, "God put two broken lives together to make a whole." And together they have formed Camp of Hope, a ministry to inner-city children in Florida.

In 2002 Margie, an inner-city mom Lori had ministered to in Phoenix, gave Lori and Jim Bakker custody of her six children: Sergio, Adriana, Maricella, Little Lori, Clarissa, and Marie. And later Margie's adult daughter gave the Bakkers legal custody of her two children, Ricky and Jennifer. Lori Graham Bakker is now the mother of eight children—and she couldn't be happier. God's blessings are more than she could ever ask.

Scriptures to Consider As You Are Trying to Escape the Pitfall of Abortion

My frame was not hidden from You,
When I was made in secret,
And skillfully wrought in the lowest parts of the earth.
Your eyes saw my substance, being yet unformed.
When as yet there were none of them. (Psalm 139:15-16)

If men fight, and hurt a woman with child, so that she gives birth prematurely, yet no harm follows, he shall surely be punished accordingly as the woman's husband imposes on him; and he shall pay as the judges determine. (Exodus 21:22)

Then the king of Egypt spoke to the Hebrew midwives . . . and he said, "When you do the duties of a midwife for the Hebrew women, and see them on the birthstools, if it is a son, then you shall kill him; but it if is a daughter, then she shall live." But the midwives feared God, and did not do as the king of Egypt commanded them, but saved the male children alive . . . Therefore God dealt well with the midwives. (Exodus 1:15–17,20)

Jesus called a little child to Him, set him in the midst of them, and said . . . "Whoever receives one little child like this in My name receives Me. Whoever causes one of these little ones who believe in Me to sin, it would be better for him if a millstone were hung around his neck, and he were drowned in the depth of the sea. Woe to the world because of offenses! For offenses must come, but woe to that man by whom the offense comes!" (Matthew 18:2–3,5–7)

Scriptures to Consider As You Are Healing from Abortion

"Come now, and let us reason together,"
Says the LORD,
"Though your sins are like scarlet,
They shall be as white as snow;
Though they are red like crimson,
They shall be as wool." (Isaiah 1:18)

He who covers his sins will not prosper,
But whoever confesses and forsakes them will have mercy.
(Proverbs 28:13)

If we confess our sins, He is faithful and just to forgive us our sins and to cleanse us from all unrighteousness. (1 John 1:9)

THE PITFALL OF ANGER

THE LIE: *"My rights are most important, and if they are violated, I am fully justified in being angry."*

After I was healed of deep-rooted unforgiveness toward my mother, I still had to deal with recurring anger toward her because of her verbal abuse every time I was with her.

"The devil is using your mother to attack you, Stormie," Mary Anne explained when I went to her office for help. "She is a willing vessel because she is controlled by those spirits. Your war is with Satan, not her."

Learning to be angry with the devil and not my mother was extremely difficult. I constantly had to remind myself who my enemy really was. Every time I was with her, I had to confess my anger to God and ask Him to help me.

We are deceived by Satan when we think, *My rights are most important, and if they are violated, I am fully justified in being angry.*

Are you holding anger against someone? List three people you might be angry with below:

The first person:

The second person:

The third person:

Now list a couple of reasons you are angry with each person. (For instance, you might feel that this person is not meeting your needs or that the person is trying to control you. Or the person might have insulted you or harmed you physically or emotionally.)

Dealing with Our Anger

The Bible does not say we should never get angry; it just sets two limits on our anger. First, we mustn't hurt someone verbally or physically. Second, we should take our anger to God quickly and not carry it around inside us so that we sin.

Anger that is managed in a healthy and responsible way is linked to a reasonable issue and is communicated in a caring and rational manner. Whenever we become angry, we have options as to how we will express that anger. Think about how you handle your anger and check the ways that apply to you:

_____ "I often suppress my anger."

_____ "I give the person the silent treatment."

_____ "I tend to be openly aggressive. Sometimes I let my anger explode into harsh words."

_____ "Sometimes I strike out against the person."

_____ "Sometimes I try to be calmly assertive. I try to state my opinion without emotion and as reasonably as possible."

_____ "Sometimes I let go of my anger."

The first four choices are unhealthy and tend to perpetuate anger and strife. For instance, suppressing your anger only buries it deeper inside you and allows it to fester. Many people dismiss "the silent treatment" as a quiet way to show displeasure. That it is, but it is also communicating anger in a way that will perpetuate tension. These first two choices are passive aggression. Passive-aggressive persons feel it is too risky to be open, so they frustrate others by subtle sabotage. They are fighting for control with the least amount of vulnerability.

We all know what being openly aggressive will do. Scripture says that "a harsh word stirs up anger" (Prov. 15:1). Yet we often allow ourselves to vent our anger in harsh words or accusations. And some of us may strike others physically. If this is so, we need to see a counselor or pastor for help.

Two of the previous options are positive. Assertive anger is being able to state your views, feelings, needs, and convictions firmly and fairly but with consideration and respect for the other person. The Bible says, "'Be angry, and do not sin': do not let the sun go down on your wrath, nor give place to the devil" (Eph. 4:26).

I know I am being assertive when I can talk to Michael about a problem without sarcasm and without bringing up old offenses.

I try to do the following:

- Make sure the issues I raise are worth raising. (I try not to waste emotional energy on trivialities.)

- Watch the tone of my voice and my body language. (No hands on the hips.)

We can also drop our anger, which is the most difficult of all. Sometimes our effort to be assertive fails—or we know it won't work. (The person will not be willing to talk through the situation, or the person is too far away or dead.) This option includes choosing to forgive—and possibly taking another approach. For instance, if your husband is a perfectionist and probably will not change, you can draw some boundaries so that you will not have to always comply with his finicky preferences.

Think of the three people you listed previously and decide how you will handle your anger toward them. If you decide to speak to them about it, note the points that are important for you to make and the way you can make these points without being angry.

The first person:

The second person:

The third person:

Now write a prayer in the space following, asking God to help you speak constructively to each person on your list. Or ask Him to help you forgive these people. (I have also found that praying for a person over a period of time helps to better understand the person and to overcome any anger.)

If you decide to drop your anger against any or all of these three people, go back to chapter 3, "The Foundation of Ongoing Forgiveness," and work through forgiveness for this person or persons.

The problem with anger, as with all other deceptions, is that if it is not dealt with properly before the Lord, it will become a spirit of anger, which will control your life. If you are susceptible to sudden angry outbursts, or if your anger level outweighs the offense and is repeated and uncontrollable, then you may have a spirit of anger. It can be inherited from a parent or picked up from observing parental outbursts when you were a child. Or if you were the victim of someone else's anger, your own unforgiveness or inability to release that memory can cause you to react violently now.

Is your anger out of control? If so, hear God speaking to you through His Word: "Let all bitterness, wrath, anger, clamor, and evil speaking be put away from you, _____, with all malice" (Eph. 4:31).

You will never find peace, restoration, and wholeness if you nurture a spirit of anger. Every single angry outburst will be a step backward from where you want to go or be, and it will keep your prayers from being answered.

If you feel you've succumbed to the pitfall of anger, speak to the devil in a loud voice of authority, saying, "Spirit of anger, I identify your presence, and I rebuke your control in the name of Jesus. I proclaim that you have no power over me, and the only one I will be angry with is *you*. I refuse to let you take life away from me by my angry outbursts. I proclaim that Jesus is Lord over my life, and He rules my mind, soul, and spirit. Anger, be gone from me in the name of Jesus." Then praise God out loud and thank Him that He is far more powerful than any spirit of deception.

Either we vent our anger toward others, which leads to destruction, or we keep it inside, making ourselves physically sick and depressed, or we direct it rightfully at the devil. The choice is clearly ours.

Scriptures to Consider When You Are Tempted to Express Your Anger in Unhealthy Ways

A man of great wrath will suffer punishment. (Proverbs 19:19)

Cease from anger, and forsake wrath;
Do not fret—it only causes harm. (Psalm 37:8)

Whoever is angry with his brother without a cause shall be in danger of the judgment. (Matthew 5:22)

A wise man fears and departs from evil,
But a fool rages and is self-confident.
A quick-tempered man acts foolishly,
And a man of wicked intentions is hated. (Prov. 14:16–17)

Make no friendship with an angry man,
And with a furious man do not go,
Lest you learn his ways,
And set a snare for your soul. (Proverbs 22:24–25)

A soft answer turns away wrath,
But a harsh word stirs up anger. (Proverbs 15:1)

He who is slow to anger is better than the mighty,
And he who rules his spirit than he who takes a city.
(Proverbs 16:32)

A fool vents all his feelings,
But a wise man holds them back. (Proverbs 29:11)

THε PITFALL OF CONFUSION

THε LIε: *"I can accept ideas that oppose God's Word."*

Years ago, I remember waking up one morning and suddenly everything seemed disjointed. I saw no purpose or future. I felt dissatisfied with everything: where I lived ("It's time to move"), my marriage ("Who is this person I'm married to?"), and my writing ("How can I possibly have anything to say?").

Why am I suddenly feeling this way? I wondered.

Then I remembered that Michael and I had attended a movie the night before that included an adulterous affair by the lonely wife of a workaholic husband. Looking back, I believe that exposure to the values in that movie, even though nothing was explicitly shown, opened the way for a spirit of confusion.

We can fall into confusion and think it's because there is something wrong with us. But it is usually because we have come under the influence of the author of confusion—Satan—who was thrown out of heaven for trying to be like God. Scripture warns us about Satan's influence in our lives: "Woe to the inhabitants of the earth and the sea! For the devil has come down to you, having great wrath, because he knows that he has a short time" (Rev. 12:12).

C.S. Lewis told of his understanding of the devil and his minions in Lewis's preface to the paperback edition of *The Screwtape Letters*. He said:

Bad angels, like bad men, are entirely practical. They have two motives. The first is fear of punishment: for as totalitarian countries have their camps for torture, so my Hell [in this book] contains deeper Hells, its "houses of correction." Their second motive is a kind of hunger. I feign that devils can, in a spiritual sense, eat one another; and us. Even in human life we have seen the passion to dominate, almost to digest, one's fellow; to make his whole intellectual and emotional life merely an extension of one's own—to hate one's hatreds and resent one's grievances and indulge one's egoism through him as well as through oneself . . .

On Earth this desire is often called "love." In Hell I feign that they recognize it as hunger. But there the hunger is more ravenous, and a fuller satisfaction is possible. There, I suggest, the stronger spirit—there are perhaps no bodies to impede the operation—can really and irrevocably suck the weaker into itself and permanently gorge its own being on the weaker's outraged individuality. It is (I feign) for this that devils desire human souls and the souls of one another.[1]

Confusion is caused by mixing Satan's darkness with God's light.

Confusion and the Worldly Perspective

Lots of confusion exists in the world today because what is bad is now considered good, and what is good is disdained. Life has become bewildering, and the only thing that breaks through the confusion is the Lord's presence and the Word of His truth.

The Bible says, "God is not the author of confusion but of peace" (1 Cor. 14:33). If He is completely in charge of every area of your life, clarity, simplicity, and peace are the immediate by-products. If not, life becomes jumbled, out of order, complex, and confusing.

However, God does sometimes use confusion to punish those who are disobedient and to destroy His enemies. He warned the Israelites about this. Before the Jewish people entered the Promised Land, Moses stopped them at the Jordan River to review the law with this new generation.

He and the Levitical priests spoke both the blessings the Israelites would receive in the Promised Land if they obeyed—and the curses that would be upon them if they disobeyed. Moses said, "The LORD will send on you cursing, confusion, and rebuke in all that you set your hand to do, until you are destroyed and until you perish quickly, because of the wickedness of your doings in which you have forsaken Me . . . The Lord will strike you with madness and blindness and confusion of heart" (Deut. 28:20,28).

God has also used confusion to destroy his enemies. Scripture is filled with these examples. God confused the languages of the arrogant people who attempted to build the tower of Babel so they could no longer communicate with one another; these people were disobeying God by trying to make a tower that would reach the heavens (Gen. 11:1–9). God promised the Israelites in the wilderness that He would help them conquer the Promised Land through confusion: "I will send My fear before you, I will cause confusion among all the people to whom you come, and will make all your enemies turn their backs to you" (Ex. 23:27).

And Isaiah prophesied great confusion in the time of the Great Tribulation:

> The city of confusion is broken down;
> Every house is shut up, so that none may go in . . .
> All joy is darkened,
> The mirth of the land is gone. (Isa. 24:10–11)

> For it is the day of the Lord's vengeance,
> The year of recompense for the cause of Zion . . .
> Its land shall become burning pitch . . .
> And He shall stretch out over it
> The line of confusion and the stones of emptiness. (Isa. 34:8–9,11)

Too many outside opinions, when you should be listening only to God's, will cause confusion. Opposing God's Word in any way will invite spirits of confusion to dwell in your life. The Bible says drinking alcohol brings confusion, but also imbibing in anything that is not of God, such as gossip, foul language, promiscuity, drugs, television, movies, and magazines tainted with worldly-mindedness.

Scripture tells us that those who worship idols "shall be ashamed / And also disgraced, all of them; / They shall go in confusion together" (Isa.

45:16). When sex, money, and power become idols in our lives, we will live in chaos and confusion.

In fact, all lust of the flesh brings confusion: "Where envy and self-seeking exist, confusion and every evil thing are there" (James 3:16).

If you are feeling confused today, take an inventory of your situation. Write down what events in your past could have caused such confusion. If you don't know, write out a prayer asking God to show you.

Eliminating the Spirit of Confusion

When confusion enters, it may cause you to make unwise or quick decisions based on a faulty frame of reference. But remember: you absolutely never have to live with confusion. Take it to God. In the space below, write out a prayer asking God to reveal if you have been disobedient in any way that has allowed a spirit of confusion to come into your life.

Now ask God to show you if any confusion in your life is from the enemy. If so, rebuke the spirit of confusion, saying "By the authority I have in Jesus Christ I command the spirit of confusion to be gone."

Then begin to worship and praise God until you are thinking clearly again. Confusion cannot coexist with God's presence and obedience to His laws. That's why worship, praise, and thanksgiving are the best weapons to dissolve it.

Scriptures to Remember When You Are Trying to Avoid the Pitfall of Confusion

For where envy and self-seeking exist, confusion and every evil thing are there. (James 3:16)

Indeed they are all worthless;
Their works are nothing;
Their molded images are wind and confusion.
(Isaiah 41:29)

But the LORD is with me as a mighty, awesome One.
Therefore my persecutors will stumble, and will not prevail.
They will be greatly ashamed, for they will not prosper.
Their everlasting confusion will never be forgotten.
(Jeremiah 20:11)

Let those be put to shame and brought to dishonor
Who seek after my life;
Let those be turned back and brought to confusion
Who plot my hurt. (Psalm 35:4)

Let them be ashamed and brought to mutual confusion
Who rejoice at my hurt;
Let them be clothed with shame and dishonor
Who exalt themselves against me. (Psalm 35:26)

THE PITFALL OF CRITICISM

THE LIE: *"I like to think I'm better than they are, but inwardly I believe they are better than I am."*

I used to be very critical of people, mentally dissecting them to see if they were better than I was, as I feared. Then I read in my Bible, "For with what judgment you judge, you will be judged; and with the same measure you use, it will be measured back to you" (Matt. 7:2). Judging people was inviting judgment upon myself.

This is the lie we want to believe when we criticize others: "I'm better than they are." But what we really fear is this: "They are better than I am." The deception we come under is thinking that anyone but God has the right to sit in judgment of another person.

Moses' sister, Miriam, who was a leader of the Hebrews, unfortunately fell into the pitfall of criticism. She and her brother Aaron criticized Moses for choosing an Ethiopian wife they didn't think was suitable for him.

God confronted Miriam and Aaron for their critical spirit. He began by showing them how wrong they were to criticize this godly man. He told them Moses was a faithful man. "I speak to him face to face, directly and not in riddles! He sees the Lord as he is. Should you not be afraid to criticize him?" (Numbers 12:8 NLT).

God didn't give Miriam time to answer His question. He quickly departed, and Miriam was left a leprous outcast.

Moses interceded for his sister (after all, she helped save him from the Pharoah's decree of death to all Hebrew baby boys). And Miriam's punishment was limited to seven days outside the camp as a leper, rather than a life of this dreaded disease.

We all need to avoid having a critical spirit.

Crowding Out a Critical Spirit

Those of us who have been abused as children often grow up to be judgmental and critical. Being torn down when we were young makes tearing someone else down to build ourselves up very appealing.

Yet constantly criticizing someone else, even in our minds, invites a critical spirit. Our every thought and word is colored by it. We eventually become cynical and completely unable to experience joy. Such criticism crowds out love in our hearts. And without love, we cannot grow emotionally.

Think about the last week. Have you been critical of someone? _____ yes; _____ no. Be completely honest about this.

If so, whom have you been critical of? Write that person's name (or the persons' names) here:

Now bring this person (or persons)—and your critical spirit toward this person (or persons)—to God. Write a prayer below, asking God to forgive you and help you overcome this critical spirit.

If you have said anything bad about this person, go to that person, and also to the person to whom you said it, and confess your error and ask for their forgiveness. You'll be amazed at how much better you'll feel, and how it will bless your relationship with those two people.

Now ask Him to give you a heart that is merciful toward others. Having a critical spirit can cut off avenues of blessing and keep you from becoming the whole person you desire to be.

Scriptures to Consider When You Are Trying to Overcome a Critical Spirit

Let none of you think evil in your heart against your neighbor. (Zechariah 8:17)

Let no corrupt word proceed out of your mouth, but what is good for necessary edification, that it may impart grace to the hearers. (Ephesians 4:29)

And above all things have fervent love for one another, for "love will cover a multitude of sins." (1 Peter 4:8)

So speak and so do as those who will be judged by the law of liberty. For judgment is without mercy to the one who has shown no mercy. Mercy triumphs over judgment. (James 2:12-13)

"He who is without sin among you, let him throw a stone at her first." (John 8:7)

THE PITFALL OF DENIAL

THE LIE: *"I know the truth, but I choose to live as if I don't."*

My father knew my mother wasn't normal, but he didn't know what to do about it. He was afraid to seek psychiatric help for fear she would be committed to a mental hospital like the ones in the horror movies he had seen in his youth. Hoping she would someday miraculously "snap out of it," he chose to ignore her problem. He lived in denial.

Denial is knowing the truth but choosing to live as if you don't. Denial is *deceiving yourself.* We say, "If I pretend this isn't happening, it will go away" or "If I tell myself this is something else, it will be."

Are you living in denial? To see if you might have fallen into this pitfall, check the statements below that apply to you:

_____ "I'm afraid to deal with _____ at the moment."

_____ "My situation is not as bad as it appears."

_____ "If I try harder, things will be all right."

_____ "My life is too messed up. Nothing will help."

_____ "I don't have a problem with alcohol or drugs. I'm able to control what I do."

_____ "My spouse or best friend drinks frequently but not excessively."

_____ "I have a secret part of my life that I feel is not necessary to reveal to anyone."

_____ "I sometimes lie about my activities to my family and friends."

_____ "Some of my family and friends have talked to me about
_____, but I don't think there is really a problem."

If you checked a couple of these statements, you might be denying a problem in your life. The last five statements relate to addictions to alcohol or drugs or indicate the possibilities of eating disorders or other problems. If you checked one of those statements, you need to see a Christian counselor or pastor to help you deal with these problems.

We are all victims of self-deception at one time or another. That's why we can never be critical of another who lives in denial.

If you live in denial about anything, you will keep coming around to the same problem over and over again. "Why doesn't this situation ever change? Why can't I ever get beyond it?" you'll ask. And the answer will be that the Spirit of truth has not been allowed to shine His light upon it.

Facing the Truth

Many people don't want to spend any time dealing with past or present problems. They often cite the passage in Scripture where the apostle Paul says we should be "forgetting those things which are behind and reaching forward to those things which are ahead" (Phil. 3:13). But what he means is that we shouldn't be living in a past or present occurrence from which we've been set free. Yet we can't be truly free if we have not brought this into the full light of God and exposed it for what it is.

Denying a problem means that it can never be solved. For instance, most addiction counselors will tell you that the first step in recovery is to get the patient out of denial.

God calls us to the truth. Scripture says, "Behold, You desire truth in the inward parts, / And in the hidden part You will make me to know wisdom" (Ps. 51:6).

I like to look at my life and work through the following introspection:

1. People have told me that I need to . . .

2. I tend to deny this because . . .

You might want to stop now and pray the prayer of the psalmist: "Search me, O God, and know my heart; / Try me, and know my anxieties; / And see if there is any wicked way in me, / And lead me in the way everlasting" (Ps. 139:23–24). Then spend a few minutes in the Lord's presence, asking Him to reveal to you any way you may be avoiding the truth.

Write down whatever He shows you in the space below.

Make No Room for Denial

God is the only one who can keep us out of denial. Write a prayer below asking God to help you break out of denial. (Be sure to ask Him to shine the light of His Word upon any area in which you are deceiving yourself.)

Then establish an accountability relationship with someone you trust. This may be your spouse, a mentor, or another same-sex friend. Choose someone who will not let you get away with self-deception. Tell this person that you want them to speak the truth in love so that you can "grow up in all things into Him who is the head—Christ" (Eph. 4:15). And vow that you will listen—truly listen—to what this person says.

Finally, you need to replace denial with the truth. As you go through this step in the book, meditate on the Scripture passages listed at the end of each pitfall. Jesus promises in John 8:32: "And you shall know the truth, and the truth shall make you free."

Scriptures to Consider When You Are Trying to Combat Denial

Behold, You desire truth in the inward parts,
And in the hidden part You will make me to know wisdom.
(Psalm 51:6)

But God shows his anger from heaven against all sinful,
wicked people who push the truth away from themselves.
(Romans 1:18 NLT).

That we should no longer be children, tossed to and fro and
carried about with every wind of doctrine, by the trickery of
men, in the cunning craftiness of deceitful plotting, but,
speaking the truth in love, may grow up in all things into
Him who is the head—Christ. (Ephesians 4:14–15)

Therefore take up the whole armor of God, that you may be
able to withstand in the evil day, and having done all, to
stand. Stand therefore, having girded your waist with truth.
(Ephesians 6:13–14)

When He, the Spirit of truth, has come, He will guide you
into all truth. (John 16:13)

The Pitfall of Depression

The Lie: *"I cannot live with my situation the way it is, and I am powerless to change it."*

*T*hirty years ago I used to wake up every morning with a familiar, gnawing ache. I would think, *That's just the way I am.* Yet since I have become emotionally healthy, I have never felt this hopelessness again. As I look back, I see that I didn't have to live like that, and I wonder how many people still live with this kind of distress. It's so familiar, and they are so used to living with these feelings, that they think it's part of their lives.

Believing we cannot live with our situation the way it is—and that we are powerless to change it—causes discouragement to settle over us like a thick fog, and we can't see any way out of the darkness. The deception is thinking that our situation is hopeless.

And we are not alone in this. Even the great prophet of God, Elijah, suffered from depression. After his enormous victory over 850 pagan prophets on Mount Carmel, Elijah is pushed into depression when the wicked queen Jezebel threatens to kill him. He runs far away into the desert, where he quivers under a solitary broom tree. "It is enough!" he said. "Now, Lord, take my life, for I am no better than my fathers!" (1 Kings 19:4).

Are you feeling as depressed as Elijah? Check the statements below that apply to you:

_____ "I frequently feel like crying."

_____ "I have difficulty thinking straight."

_____ "I'm not hungry and do not feel like eating regular meals."

_____ "I wake up at night and have difficulty going back to sleep."

_____ "I have trouble finishing a task."

_____ "I have lost interest in hobbies and other activities I enjoy."

_____ "I feel sad much of the time."

_____ "I have little hope for the future."

_____ "I am tired and have little energy."

_____ "I sometimes wish I could stay in bed instead of getting up."

_____ "I get upset easily."

If you checked the first five statements, and these symptoms have persisted for two weeks or so, you may be experiencing depression. I battled depression until I was in my early thirties. Now when I'm threatened by depression, I recognize that something is out of order in my life or my mind, and I immediately take it to the Lord.

Defeating Depression

If you struggle with occasional bouts of depression, or are depressed right now, I suggest that you go before the Lord and ask the same questions I ask:

1. Is there any physical problem that could be causing this?

Many of us wonder why Elijah would be so depressed. He had just experienced God's great miracle of igniting a fire supernaturally on a wood pile that had been wetted down three times and was surrounded by a man-made moat. He and the Lord won the victory over Baal and his humiliated prophets, who had spent all day asking Baal to show his greatness by also igniting a fire.

Yet if we crawl into Elijah's skin for a while, we will probably understand his depression. Elijah was exhausted after this confrontation with the 450 prophets of Baal and the 400 prophets of Asherah. The odds were overwhelming. The day was long and hot. The crowd was watching and probably jeering and poking fun at this solitary prophet of God. Elijah was worn out from standing up for God while God's other prophets cowered in the caves.

Then Jezebel, the most wicked queen in the Bible, sent a messenger to confront him with her wrath. And since she was queen, she was not alone. The power of the nation of Israel stood behind her. Now do you understand Elijah's depression?

Do you feel overwhelmed as Elijah did? You may be tired from overwork or stress or difficult times, like a child's rebellion or a husband's demands. Or you might be suffering from PMS (premenstrual syndrome), diabetes, or a nutritional shortage, like an iron deficiency. Check with your doctor if any symptoms like headaches or fatigue accompany your depression.

2. Is there anyone or any circumstance causing this depression?

Weight Watchers, the popular and proven weight loss program, asks its members to journal each day's food intake. As the week progresses, people realize how many calories they have been consuming—and they begin to adjust their intake.

Journal your past week. What important events occurred during this last seven days?

Now look over those events. Could any of them have triggered depression? If so, list that event or events below.

Then take the same inventory of the week before. What events occurred during that previous seven-day period?

Could any of these events have triggered depression? If so, list that event or events below.

In his best-selling book *The Lies We Believe*, Dr. Chris Thurman suggests that we look at our lives through the context of the ABC approach developed by psychologist Albert Ellis:

- *A* represents the event that happened to you (the ones that you listed in your journal).

- *B* represents "self-talk," what you mentally told yourself about the event.

- *C* represents your emotional reaction to that "self-talk." It can be anything from joy to despair.[1]

Take one of the events that might have contributed to depression and put it through this ABC approach:

A (Event one):
In Elijah's case this would be Jezebel's threat.

B (Your self-talk):
Elijah probably thought, *Jezebel, oh no! I thought I had won this victory. Now I have the queen after me—and her entire army.*

C (Your emotional reaction to the event):
Elijah's emotional reaction was fear, which led to his depression. He was rough and rugged, but he was also emotionally sensitive. And he isolated himself from everyone. He told his servant to stay in Beersheba, a town in Judah, and Elijah went alone into the arid desert.

Now you may have identified the source of your depression—or you still may be unsure. I always continue with my inventory by asking, is there any sin I haven't confessed?

3. Is there any sin I haven't confessed?

Sometimes the cause of depression is external (being exposed to something ungodly). Sometimes it is an attack of the devil (especially when God is doing a powerful work in your life). But most of the time wrong thinking or a wrong action (an inappropriate response to a person or situation) causes our depression.

Look at the situations you identified on the previous two pages. Have you missed the mark in these situations? If so, list those ways below:

Now take these reactions to the Lord by writing a prayer. Ask for His forgiveness and for Him to help you right the wrong.

4. Have I prayed about my depression?

Remember that God is on your side and the devil is your enemy. Pastor Jack taught me, "You have to wait at Jesus' feet through the darkness. There is no night so long or so dark but that if you stay at the feet of the Lord; He will take care of it in the morning." Psalm 30:5 says, "Weeping may endure for a night, / But joy comes in the morning."

If you wake up in the night with your heart pounding in fear or depression, get up immediately and go to your prayer closet and pray and read the Word. Go back to sleep when you can, and then continue praying the next day. Often when people don't get an immediate answer to their prayers, they stop turning to God and try to work it out on their own. Don't do that.

Stop right now and write a prayer, asking God to help you dismiss the negative thoughts leading to your depression. Commit yourself to Him and ask Him to help you to focus on the positive parts of your life.

5. What lies am I listening to?

In his book Chris Thurman helps readers identify the lies in their lives. These lies, he says, are the number-one cause of our unhappiness.

Check the lies below that you might be accepting as truth:

_____ "I must have everyone's love and approval."

_____ "My unhappiness is somebody else's fault."

_____ "I am only as good as what I do."

_____ "Life should be fair."

_____ "If our marriage takes such hard work, we must not be right for each other."

_____ "Depression, anger, and anxiety are signs of a weak faith in God."

Then test these lies against Scripture in the next step of this process.

6. Which of God's promises can I quote aloud to sum up His perspective as it relates to me or my situation?

"I must have everyone's love and approval." We don't need anyone else's approval. Scripture says:

Behold what manner of love the Father has bestowed on us, that we should be called children of God! . . . Beloved, now we are children of God; and it has not yet been revealed what we shall be, but we know that when He is revealed, we shall be like Him, for we shall see Him as He is. (1 John 3:1–2)

The apostle Paul knew he didn't need anyone else's approval, only God's. He said, "Am I now trying to win the approval of men, or of God? Or am I trying to please men? If I were still trying to please men, I would not be a servant of Christ" (Gal. 1:10 NIV).

We do not have to have everyone's love and approval.

"My unhappiness is somebody else's fault." The Bible tells us to accept responsibility for our own actions. Scripture says:

Do all things without complaining and disputing, that you may become blameless and harmless, children of God without fault in the midst of a crooked and perverse generation, among whom you shine as lights in the world. (Phil. 2:14–15)

Be honest with yourself. Have you contributed to your unhappiness? If so, list those ways below:

"I am only as good as what I do." God sees us as important for who we are, not what we do. Scripture says:

What is man that You are mindful of him,
And the son of man that You visit him?
For You have made him a little lower than the angels,
And You have crowned him with glory and honor. (Ps. 8:4–5)

If I am naturally just "a little lower than the angels, "I'm okay in and of myself.

"Life should be fair." God never promised us a rose garden. Instead, trouble is referred to 143 times in the Bible. Scripture says: "There is something else meaningless that occurs on earth: righteous men who get what the wicked deserve, and wicked men who get what the righteous deserve. This too, I say, is meaningless" (Eccl. 8:14 NIV).

Life isn't fair, but God is good. He walks with us through our troubles and turns bad into good (Rom. 8:28).

"If our marriage takes such hard work, we must not be right for each other." Scripture says: "But those who marry will face many troubles in this life" (1 Cor. 7:28 NIV). That doesn't sound very encouraging, but since life is tough, anyone—married or unmarried—will face trouble. And overcoming trouble takes hard work.

"Depression, anger, and anxiety are signs of a weak faith in God." Elijah certainly did not have a weak faith in God. If he had, he wouldn't have challenged the 850 pagan prophets to this Herculean contest. Nor would he have appeared with Moses and Jesus in the Transfiguration. If Elijah was depressed, we should not feel guilty if we are sometimes anxious.

Scripture acknowledges anger as well. The Bible says: "In your anger do not sin" (Eph. 4:26 NIV). That's the instruction that Christians need to remember.

7. How much have I praised, worshiped, and thanked God in the midst of my depression?
Being depressed is a sign that your personality has focused on itself. Elijah didn't stop to think of others—or to see if other prophets were hiding somewhere in Israel. He ran, most of the way by himself.

God saved Elijah by sending an angel to feed him; the Lord also helped Elijah to find rest in sleep. Then He appeared to Elijah at Horeb, the mountain of God. The Almighty God spoke to Elijah in a still, small voice. Finally, Elijah focused on God, rather than on himself. And the Lord sent Elijah back into ministry.

One of the healthiest steps away from depression is to focus on God through praise. Stop everything you're doing and write a prayer of praise to God in the space on the bottom of the next page. Be sure to give Him thanks for walking through depression beside you, vow to refuse to give depression a hold on your life, and tell Him how much you love Him.

Finally, when you journey through a sad time, read through the Scriptures on the next page. Star the ones that are most meaningful to you and copy one or two on an index card to place in your purse or on a mirror. Never forget Paul's insight as he walked with the Lord through discouraging times: "And we know that all things work together for good to those who love God, to those who are the called according to His purpose" (Rom. 8:28).

When Nothing Helps

If you've asked yourself these questions and done all that's been suggested and are still deeply depressed, then you need to seek out a Christian counselor. If you can't get an immediate appointment, make yourself get up each day and do at least two things. Wash the dishes and make the beds. Or pull some weeds in the yard and wash your car. Whatever it is, do it and don't worry about anything else. Then take your Bible, sit down with the Lord, and take comfort in the fact that your life has some order and you have accomplished something.

Scripture says: "Anxiety in the heart of man causes depression, / But a good word makes it glad" (Prov. 12:25). Because of Jesus, you can win over depression.

Scriptures to Consider When You Feel Depressed

The LORD has appeared of old to me, saying:
"Yes, I have loved you with an everlasting love;
Therefore with lovingkindness I have drawn you.
Again I will build you, and you shall be rebuilt."
(Jeremiah 31: 3–4)

I can do all things through Christ who strengthens me.
(Philippians 4:13)

Being confident of this very thing, that He who has begun a good work in you will complete it until the day of Jesus Christ. (Philippians 1:6)

Therefore, if anyone is in Christ, he is a new creation; old things have passed away; behold, all things have become new. (2 Corinthians 5:17)

For we are His workmanship, created in Christ Jesus for good works, which God prepared beforehand that we should walk in them. (Ephesians 2:10)

Be anxious for nothing, but in everything by prayer and supplication, with thanksgiving, let your requests be made known to God; and the peace of God, which surpasses all understanding, will guard your hearts and minds through Christ Jesus. (Philippians 4:6–7)

THE PITFALL OF ENVY

THE LIE: *"I need and deserve to have what he (or she) has."*

One day as I read the Bible, the Lord spoke to my heart through a verse that says, "For where envy and self-seeking exist, confusion and every evil thing are there" (James 3:16). It was as if the Lord pointed to me and said, "You have confusion in your life right now because of the envy and self-seeking in your heart."

How embarrassed I felt. Me? Have envy? But I came to realize that constantly measuring myself against others was the seed from which envy grows.

This is the lie we believe when we are envious of someone: "I need and deserve to have what he or she has." The truth is that everything we have comes from God. To have sorrow, discontent, or ill will over someone else's possessions or advantages is to reject what God is able to give us. The deception of envy is thinking that God doesn't have enough to go around.

Envy is the ultimate idolatry, and idolatry is the root of envy. The Bible says we are to put to death "covetousness, which is idolatry" (Col. 3:5) because it will undermine the purposes of God in our lives.

Do you tend to envy others? Check the statements below that apply to you:

_____ "I attended a party at a friend's house. When I got home, our house looked shabby. I feel bad because I don't have a house like my friend's."

_____ "I sometimes want a new car because my neighbor just got one."

_____ "_____ is so smart. Everything at work is so easy for her (him). Why can't I be that smart?"

_____ "I still feel that my mother (father) loves my sister (brother) more than me."

_____ "When my friend at work got a promotion, I couldn't help feeling a little sad. I wish it had been me."

_____ "_____ is so outgoing and friendly. I feel bad about myself; I wish I could be like her."

_____ "My neighbor's kids always seem to do everything right. I wish mine were like that."

_____ "_____ always has such beautiful clothes. I wish I had clothes like hers."

If you checked more than a couple of statements, you have fallen into the pitfall of envy.

Free Yourself from Envy

To be free of envy you should work through the following inventory of your life, just as I did.

1. Take stock of everything God has given me and be thankful for it.
   Take a moment right now to do such an inventory in the space below. God has given me . . .

Now take another moment and write a prayer below to thank God for the items you mentioned:

2. Come to terms with my limitations and strictly avoid comparing myself to others.

The Bible says that we are "fearfully and wonderfully made" (Ps. 139:14). God sees our weaknesses: He searches us and knows us; He knows our sitting down and our rising up; He is acquainted with all our ways. Yet He still loves us.

If the Almighty God can love us—weaknesses and all—we should be able to accept ourselves as we are.

List three of your weaknesses below:

Now write a prayer, asking God to help you accept these weaknesses. Where you can change them, ask God to help you do so. Where you can't, ask God to help you accept them. The prayer of Alcoholics Anonymous is so true: "God, grant me serenity to accept the things I cannot change; courage to change the things I can; and wisdom to know the difference."

3. Be thankful to God for other people's talents and gifts.

Think of three people whom you admire greatly. Write their names below and explain why you admire them. Ask God to show you if there is any envy in your admiration. If so, ask Him to set you free from it.

Now write a prayer, thanking God for these people's talents and gifts. (Let the Lord know that because He created you, He knows what will fulfill you. Ask His forgiveness if you have coveted anything these three

people have. Acknowledge that what He has for you is better than anything you could covet for yourself.)

4. List my own talents and remind myself of my calling from God.

Before you argue that you have no talents, remember that God has
given each of us some talents. No one in the parable of the talents (Matt.
25:14–30) was without talent; there were just varying degrees of the Lord's
blessings.

Now write a prayer, thanking God for your talents and asking Him to
help you know how He wants you to use them:

Finally, list those talents below and note how each of them could be
used:

Talent One:
It could be used by . . .

Talent Two:
It could be used by . . .

Talent Three:
It could be used by . . .

Envy will put great limitations on your life. If you are envious of what someone has, you will either never have that yourself, or you will get it and won't be satisfied by it. The Bible asks, "Who is able to stand before jealousy?" (Prov. 27:4). Whether in you or directed at you, envy is evil. Satan fell from heaven because he wanted what God had. It will be your downfall, too.

Focus on making the apostle Paul's attitude your attitude. He said, "For we brought nothing into this world, and it is certain we can carry nothing out. And having food and clothing, with these we shall be content" (1 Tim. 6:7–8).

Scriptures to Consider If You Are
Tempted by the Pitfall of Envy

And He said to them, "Take heed and beware of covetousness, for one's life does not consist in the abundance of the things he possesses." (Luke 12:15)

But fornication and all uncleanness or covetousness, let it not even be named among you, as is fitting for saints. (Ephesians 5:3)

For where there are envy, strife, and divisions among you, are you not carnal and behaving like mere men? (1 Corinthians 3:3)

You shall not covet your neighbor's house . . . nor anything that is your neighbor's. (Exodus 20:17)

Let your conduct be without covetousness; be content with such things as you have. (Hebrews 13:5-6)

A sound heart is life to the body,
But envy is rottenness to the bones. (Proverbs 14:30)

Not that I speak in regard to need, for I have learned in whatever state I am, to be content: I know how to be abased, and I know how to abound. (Philippians 4:11)

Love suffers long and is kind; love does not envy; love does not parade itself, is not puffed up. (1 Corinthians 13:4)

THE PITFALL OF FEAR

THE LIE: *"God is not able to keep me and all that I care about safe."*

I have heard it said many times that F-E-A-R stands for False Evidence Appearing Real. But some fears are also warranted. We will look at both in this chapter, beginning with false evidence.

False Evidence Appearing Real

One of the biggest fears for anyone who has been emotionally damaged is fear of the opinion of others. Our fears tell us, "People won't like me when they find out what I'm really like." But Isaiah 51:7 tells us, "Do not fear the reproach of men, / Nor be afraid of their insults."

What unrealistic fears do you have? For instance you may fear heights when you are actually safe inside a skywalk above a busy downtown street. List your unrealistic fears in the space below:

Warranted Fears

Some of our fears are warranted. In the coming years Americans will all worry about terrorist attacks as our government continually alerts us to the possibilities of another attack like September 11, 2001. We also naturally worry about our safety if we live in an area where there is a high crime rate. Some of us worry when we are taking a long car trip. Could our car break down or could there be a torrential rainstorm that would make driving dangerous?

List your natural fears in the space below:

What to Do When You Are Afraid

The opposite of fear is faith, and we usually interpret the circumstances of our lives through one or the other. Here are four ways you can overcome your fear with God's help.

1. Confess your fear to the Lord and ask Him to free you from it.

Don't deny your fear. Instead, take the unwarranted fears you listed above to God and ask for deliverance. Write that prayer below, remembering to first confess your fear as sin and ask God to forgive you for it. Ask Him to strengthen your faith in Him, and then command the spirit of fear to be gone in the name of Jesus.

2. Check to see if there is, in fact, a very real danger, and do what you can to remedy the situation.

Look at the realistic fears you listed above. Take two of these fears and analyze how you can remedy them. For instance, if you are afraid of someone entering your house, you might reinforce your doors with bolts or you might hire a security service. Your fear can cause you to take precautionary measures in order to keep you from harm.

My fear is _____.

I can take the following step or steps to prevent this fear from happening:

My fear is _____.

I can take the following action to prevent this fear from happening:

3. Commit to trust the Lord unquestioningly for seven days, then extend that period to a month—and then the rest of your life.

In Psalm 91 God promises to protect us. But there is a prerequisite to feeling His protection: you must abide in the shadow of the Almighty by saying, "He is my refuge and my fortress; / My God, in Him I will trust" (v. 2).

Determine to trust the Lord completely for the next seven days. As you do so, insert your name in the spaces below from Psalm 91:

> Surely He shall deliver you, _____, from the snare of the
>   fowler
> And from the perilous pestilence.
> He shall cover you, _____, with His feathers,
> And under His wings you, _____, shall take refuge.
>   (vv. 3–4)

These passages describe God as a caring parent, like a mother bird who is protecting her beloved baby. Feel God's wings around you, protecting you from terror by night and the destruction that might appear at noonday.

Then think about His promises to you because you have made the Lord your refuge. Insert your name in the blank spaces.

> No evil shall befall you, _____,
> Nor shall any plague come near your dwelling;
> For He shall give His angels charge over you, _____,
> To keep you in all your ways.
> They shall bear you up in their hands,
> Lest you, _____, dash your foot against a stone. (vv. 10–13)

And hear God speak to you directly through this paraphrase of verses 14–16:

> Because _____ has set her love upon Me,
> I will set _____on high, because she has known My name.
> _____ shall call upon Me, and I will answer her.
> I will be with her in trouble;
> I will deliver her and honor her.
> With long life I will satisfy her,
> And show her My salvation.

Read through these verses in the coming seven days or read through all of Psalm 91 each day. Then highlight your favorite promise or promises and say them throughout the day. When you store them in your heart, they will crowd out fear. The only fear you are to have is the fear of God, a respect for God's authority and power.

4. Worship the Lord out loud.

Praise is your greatest weapon against fear, so use it with great force. Clap your hands, put one of your favorite promises in Psalm 91 to a familiar tune, and sing it over and over again. Speak praises to God, thanking Him for His great love.

> As you do so, remember God's promise to you in Isaiah:
> Fear not, for I *am* with you, _____;
> Be not dismayed, for I *am* your God.
> I will strengthen you,
> Yes, I will help you,
> I will uphold you, _____, with My righteous right hand.
> (Isaiah 41:10)

No matter what has happened to you or is happening in the world around you, God promises to protect you as you walk with Him. Pray that He will and trust Him to do so.

Scriptures to Consider When You Are Afraid

Be strong and of good courage, do not fear nor be afraid of them; for the LORD your God, He is the One who goes with you. He will not leave you nor forsake you.
(Deuteronomy 31:6)

The LORD is my light and my salvation;
Whom shall I fear? (Psalm 27:1)

Say to those who are fearful-hearted,
"Be strong, do not fear!
Behold, your God will come with vengeance,
With the recompense of God;
He will come and save you." (Isaiah 35:4)

"Do no fear, little flock, for it is your Father's good pleasure to give you the kingdom." (Jesus' words in Luke 12:32)

There is no fear in love; but perfect love casts out fear, because fear involves torment. But he who fears has not been made perfect in love. (1 John 4:18)

"Do not fear any of those things which you are about to suffer. Indeed, the devil is about to throw some of you into prison, that you may be tested, and you will have tribulation ten days. Be faithful until death, and I will give you the crown of life." (Jesus' words in Revelation 2:10)

25

THE PITFALL OF LUST

THE FIRST LIE: *"It doesn't hurt to think about it if I'm not actually going to do anything."*

THE SECOND LIE: *"This won't really hurt anyone else, and I will be truly happy."*

Lust is an excessive desire to gratify any of the senses, but I am referring here to sexual desire, a specific spirit that comes to destroy your life by tempting you to think and do something you have already made a decision not to do.

Every lustful act begins as a simple thought. We are deceived if we think we are too strong or too good to ever be tempted. The Bible says, "He who trusts in his own heart is a fool, / But whoever walks wisely will be delivered" (Prov. 28:26).

We are told that King David was a man after God's own heart. Yet he fell into the pitfall of lust. Let's follow his plunge as we learn how to avoid this pitfall.

We all know David from the courageous story of his killing the giant Goliath with a slingshot—when no one in Saul's formidable army would accept the giant's challenge. And we all know that David was a just, dynamic ruler of Israel.

Unfortunately, we also know that David sinned when he coveted Uriah's wife, Bathsheba. His lust was aroused as he looked from the rooftop of his palace and saw this beautiful woman bathing.

As you think about your own temptations, look at where David failed. First he was where he wasn't supposed to be; he should have been with his troops at Rabbah. Instead he stayed home. And he probably imagined what it would be like to be with a gorgeous woman. He fell prey to the first lie of lust: "It doesn't hurt to think about it if I'm not actually going to do anything."

But that wasn't true for David, any more than it's true for us. So he sent for Bathsheba, instead of fleeing from the temptation. And he bought into the second lie: "This won't really hurt anyone else, and I will be truly happy."

Think about your own situation. Mentally check the following statements that apply to you:

_____ "I sometimes think of this person and imagine what it would be like to be near him / her."

_____ "There are moments when I know I'm in a situation that could be tempting."

_____ "Instead of fleeing the situation, I remain there."

_____ "I think I'm too strong a Christian to give in to the temptation I feel."

If you mentally checked these statements, you probably have been tempted by lust. When you are tempted in this way, you need to remember God's will for you. Hear God speaking to you directly by inserting your name in the blanks.

For this is the will of God, your sanctification: that you, _____, should abstain from sexual immorality; that you, _____, should know how to possess your own vessel in sanctification and honor, not in passion of lust, like the Gentiles who do not know God. (paraphrase of 1 Thess. 4:3–5)

Each of us needs to take a mental inventory of our emotions every so often. And if we come in contact with someone for whom we feel a strong attraction, we need to immediately rebuke the devil. If you checked some of the statements in the inventory on this page, write a rebuke of this temptation and its originator in the space below. (Be sure to bind Satan in Jesus' name and assert that you want no part of this sin against God.)

Now go before the Lord in prayer. Write your petition in the space below. (Confess your attraction to this person and ask for God's forgiveness. Ask Him to help you understand why Satan thinks he can attack you in this area. End by asking Him to help you blot out these thoughts from your mind.)

As you try to conquer lustful thoughts, remember God's promise to you:

No temptation has overtaken you, _____, except such as is common to man; but God is faithful, who will not allow you, _____, to be tempted beyond what you are able, but with the temptation will also make the way of escape, that you, _____, may be able to bear it. (1 Cor. 10:13)

Unfortunately, some of us have already fallen prey to this pitfall. David did—and he went beyond adultery to having Uriah killed once it was obvious that Bathsheba had become pregnant—while her husband was far away with David's army.

After the Fall

David hid his adultery with Bathsheba for a year, until the prophet Nathan confronted him. "Why have you despised the commandment of the LORD?" he asked David. "Now therefore, the sword shall never depart from your house" (2 Sam. 12:9–10).

God punished David. The prophet predicted God's sentence: Bathsheba's baby died; one of David's sons, Amnon, raped his half-sister, Tamar; another son, Absalom, killed Amnon because of this sin against his sister; and Absalom soon plotted to overthrow his father, David. Sounds like a soap opera, doesn't it? The second lie associated with the pitfall of adultery was certainly a lie in David's case. He may have thought, *This won't really hurt anyone else, and I will be truly happy,* but the future proved him wrong.

Just as God punished David, He will punish us if we fall into the pitfall of lust. Scripture says, "Do not be deceived, God is not mocked; for whatever a man sows, that he will also reap" (Gal. 6:7).

And the Lord will also forgive our sin, just as He forgave David's. God does not, however, take away the consequences of our actions.

If you have acted on the spirit of lust, you need to walk through the steps David took in Psalm 51, which is David's cry to God after he committed this sin.

A Psalm of Confession

King David could have denied Nathan's accusation and ordered the prophet's death. Instead, David admitted his sin and acknowledged it to the Lord. Follow David's example by inserting your name in David's confession:

> For I, _____, acknowledge my transgressions,
> And my sin is always before me.
> Against You, You only, have I sinned,
> And done this evil in Your sight. (vv. 3–4)

Most of us don't think that our sins are against God. Yet He does suffer from our transgressions. Even today people cite David's transgression as proving that adultery isn't wrong. David knew he had sinned against God—and we also need to admit this.

Then David pleads with God as you might also want to do:

> Create in me a clean heart, O God,
> And renew a steadfast spirit within me. (vv. 10–11)

Like David we must ask God to cleanse us from within, giving us a new heart and a new spiritual zest for Him. Sin was the exception in David's life—not a pattern that continued into the future.

God forgave David. He continued to think of him as a man after His own heart. And God will forgive you if you are truly repentant.

At the end of this psalm David makes two promises to God. Consider them for yourself:

Then I, _____, will teach transgressors Your ways,
And sinners shall be converted to You . . .
O Lord, open my lips,
And my mouth shall show forth Your praise. (vv. 13–15)

Someone who is truly repentant can help others who seem to be straying toward the same pitfall. And you can too. Ask God to show you how you can serve Him in this way.

And if you have acted on a spirit of lust, you need to receive deliverance. Get help. Go to a counselor, a Christian therapist, a pastor, or a strong believer who will keep your confidence. Confess your sin.

Then experience the joy of being forgiven. David wrote Psalm 32 to express his renewed relationship with God:

Surely in a flood of great waters
They shall not come near me,
You are my hiding place;
You shall preserve me from trouble;
You shall surround me with songs of deliverance. (vv. 6-7,
    paraphrased)

At the end of the psalm David celebrated God's blessedness in forgiving him—and us. He tells us to:

Be glad in the LORD and rejoice, you righteous;
And shout for joy, all you upright in heart! (v. 11)

Scriptures to Consider When You Are Tempted by Lust

The righteousness of the upright will deliver them,
But the unfaithful will be caught by their lust. (Proverbs 11:6)

I say then: Walk in the Spirit, and you shall not fulfill the lust of the flesh. (Galatians 5:16)

For this is the will of God, your sanctification: that you should abstain from sexual immorality; that each of you should know how to possess his own vessel in sanctification and honor, not in passion of lust, like the Gentiles who do not know God. (1 Thessalonians 4:3–5)

For he who sows to his flesh will of the flesh reap corruption, but he who sows to the Spirit will of the Spirit reap everlasting life. (Galatians 6:8)

26

THE PITFALL OF LYING

THE LIE: *"A lie will make things better for me."*

I learned to lie as a child because I felt that the consequences of telling the truth were too great. I was so embarrassed about my life that lying to others was far more tolerable than admitting to what was real. Our family lived in great poverty in a ramshackle house behind a gas station, so I either lied about where I lived or, when possible, evaded the question altogether.

The deception of lying is thinking that a lie will make things better for you. Actually it does the opposite. Telling a lie means that you have aligned yourself with the spirit of lies, who is Satan. *Lying means you have just given the devil a piece of your heart.* The more you lie, the greater his hold on you, and once you are bound by a lying spirit, you won't be able to stop yourself from lying.

People who have been physically or emotionally abused learn to lie to protect themselves or to feel better about themselves. Yet the Bible says, "Getting treasures by a lying tongue / Is the fleeting fantasy of those who seek death" (Prov. 21:6).

A Biblical Liar

Most Christians think of Abraham as the father of the Hebrew people and the spiritual father of all Christians because of his deep faith in God. But Abraham had his spiritual struggles, and he fell into the pitfall of lying. He bought into the deception that "a lie will make things better for me."

And he told the same lie twice—in two different situations. Abraham was married to a beautiful woman named Sarah who was his half-sister; they had the same father but different mothers. Abraham told a half-lie.

He first misrepresented Sarah as his sister, not his wife, to the Pharaoh and the princes of Egypt (Gen. 12:10–20) because Abraham was afraid that the Egyptians might try to kill him so they could marry his beautiful wife. Abraham did not trust God to keep him safe; instead he lied to protect himself.

Pharaoh believed Abraham's lie and took Sarah into his palace. While Sarah was going through the time of preparation to become the wife of the ruler, God intervened. He sent plagues to stop Pharaoh from marrying Sarah.

Abraham was caught lying—and he was expelled from Egypt with his wife and all that he had.

You'd think Abraham would have learned his lesson. But many years later we see him telling the same lie. By giving into this temptation again he risks turning a sinful act into a sinful pattern of lying, just as we do when we repeat a lie over and over again.

Abraham and his family journeyed to Gerar, and again he was worried that he might be killed so King Abimelech could marry his beautiful wife. Again his faith wavered. He told the king that Sarah was his sister, so the king sent for her—but again God intervened (Gen. 20).

When Abraham finally repented of his sin, the Lord answered his prayer for a son. He and Sarah had never been able to have a child, but God didn't bless them with an heir until Abraham repented of the sin of lying.

This is the same son that God later asked Abraham to sacrifice to Him. By this time Abraham's faith in God had matured so that he did as God commanded. And God restrained Abraham's knife at the last minute. His son Isaac lived to father the great Hebrew nation.

Abraham had to deal with his lies before he could have the blessing of a child. And it's the same for you and me. We have to deal with the lies in our lives before God can bless us.

If you are falling into the pit of lying, you must confess every lie to God. Take an inventory of the last week, then the last month, in the space below. Mention the lies that you have told:

The last week:

The last month:

Now look further. Is there a lie you have been telling over and over again for years? If so, write it in the space below:

Read back over the list of your previous lies and confess each one to God as you do. Then write a prayer in the space below, asking God to forgive you and cleanse you of all evil.

Now say directly to Satan, "Satan, I refuse to be a part of your deception and evil, and I command your lying spirit to be gone in the name of Jesus."

Finally, immerse yourself in God's truth, His Word. Ask God to show you any other lie that you are speaking or living. Lying keeps you from enjoying healthy relationships.

Proverbs 26:28 says, "A lying tongue hates its victims, and flattery causes ruin" (NLT). And lying separates you from the presence of the Lord: "He who tells lies shall not continue in my presence" (Ps. 101:7). You can't have emotional health and happiness without the presence of God in your life.

Vow to make the truth of Proverbs a part of your life in the future by writing your name in the Scripture below:

Let not mercy and truth forsake you, _____;
Bind them around your neck,
Write them on the tablet of your heart,
And so find favor and high esteem
In the sight of God and man. (Prov. 3:3–4)

Scriptures to Consider When You Are
Trying to Overcome Lying

You will destroy those who tell lies.
The Lord detests murderers and deceivers. (Psalm 5:6 TLB)

A righteous man hates lying,
But a wicked man is loathsome and comes to shame.
(Proverbs 13:5)

Therefore, putting away lying, "Let each one of you speak truth
with his neighbor," for we are members of one another.
(Ephesians 4:25).

Lying lips are an abomination to the LORD,
But those who deal truthfully are His delight.
(Proverbs 12:22)

These six things the LORD hates,
Yes, seven are an abomination to Him:
A proud look,
A lying tongue,
Hands that shed innocent blood,
A heart that devises wicked plans,
Feet that are swift in running to evil,
A false witness who speaks lies,
And one who sows discord among brethren.
(Proverbs 6:16–19)

THE PITFALL OF PERFECTIONISM

THE LIE: *"I can be perfect."*

People who are part of the entertainment industry in Hollywood, as I was, try to look perfect every time they walk out of the house. I certainly tried to do that, and I fell into the pit of perfectionism. I was afraid of marriage because I thought I wouldn't be a perfect wife. I was afraid to have children because I thought I wouldn't be a perfect mom. For years I wouldn't write anything for people to see because I knew what I wrote wasn't perfect. I was trying to be perfect in order to be acceptable to myself and to others; but in reality, the more perfect we try to make ourselves, the more uncomfortable we make the people around us.

The deception of perfectionism is in thinking that anyone other than God can ever be perfect.

Be Ye Perfect?

I once wrote a magazine article in which I said, "God never asks us to be perfect; He simply asks us to take steps of obedience." Someone wrote to me afterward, saying, "How can you say that when Matthew 5:48 clearly says, 'You shall be perfect, just as your Father in heaven is perfect'"?

In a responding article, I wrote that the definition of *perfect* in the *New World Dictionary* is "complete in all respects, flawless, faultless, without defect, in a condition of complete excellence."[1] If we use this definition, Jesus is saying "You must be faultless, without defect, and completely excellent!" That's impossible!

So what did Jesus mean when He said, "Be perfect, therefore, as your heavenly Father is perfect" (Matt. 5:48 NIV)? It's explained a few verses earlier, where Jesus said, "You have heard that it was said, 'You shall love your neighbor and hate your enemy.' But I say to you, love your enemies, bless those who curse you, do good to those who hate you, and pray for those who spitefully use you and persecute you" (Matt. 5:43–44). The passage goes on to say that if you love as God loves, you shall be perfect, just as your Father in heaven is perfect. In other words, if we are motivated in all we do by love for God, which overflows into love for others, we shall be perfected. *Being perfect has to do with the condition of the heart.*

A heart that is pure in love toward God is a heart that desires to obey Him. God knows our actions can never be 100 percent perfect. That's why He sent Jesus. But our hearts can be perfect even if our actions are not.

We who were abused as children are already painfully aware of our imperfections. We need to know that God doesn't expect us to be perfect in *performance* but perfect *in our hearts.*

Do you struggle with perfectionism? Check the statements below to see if this is a pitfall for you:

_____ "I usually think I could have done something better."

_____ "I always expect the best of myself—and of others."

_____ "I feel bad about myself if my house is not perfect."

_____ "I find it very hard to take criticism of my work."

_____ "If I can't do something well, I don't do it at all."

_____ "I feel ashamed if I show weakness or foolish behavior."

_____ "In my experience, if you want something done right, you have to do it yourself."

_____ "I get upset when things don't go as planned."

_____ "I think about my failures much more than my successes."

_____ "I sometimes think other people dwell on my faults, rather than my strengths."

How many statements did you check? If you checked more than a couple, you have perfectionist tendencies. Actually many of us fall prey to this pitfall, especially those of us who have been abused.

Why do we fall into this pit? Most perfectionists share three common characteristics: dichotomous thinking, unrealistic goals, and lowered self-esteem.

Dichotomous Thinking

Dichotomous thinking is either-or thinking. I am either perfect or imperfect (which often makes me feel like a failure). I am either a good mother or a bad mother. A good wife or a bad wife. A good writer or a bad writer. Everything is either black or white. There is no in-between.

This leads to several distorted patterns, as Dr. David Stoop points out in his book, *Hope for the Perfectionist*.[2] Dichotomous thinking is reflected in the self-test statement: "If I can't do something well, I don't do it at all." A friend of mine refuses to learn to play golf because she has always been uncoordinated and knows that she probably cannot play well. She's sacrificed some enjoyable moments with her husband by being a perfectionist.

Perfectionists also practice *maximizing* and *minimizing*. They maximize their failures and minimize their successes. Some of us never truly hear our husbands say, "You look great." Instead we dwell on the moments when we have a "bad hair day." If you checked the statement "I think about my failures much more than my successes," you are falling into this trap.

Finally, perfectionists tend to give *a negative attribution to other people's motives or behaviors*. They focus on another person's seemingly negative tone of voice as a sign of disapproval. Actually they are attributing their own negative feelings about themselves to another person. If you checked the statement "I sometimes think other people dwell on my faults, rather than my strengths," you are falling into this trap.

Perfectionists also tend to set unrealistic goals for themselves and others.

Unrealistic Goals

While a healthy achiever rates only her *performance*, a perfectionist is rating *herself*. I know someone who tries so hard to have a clean, immaculate house that she alienates her children. Her goal—a perfect environment—is impossible in a family with kids. And actually in any home. If you checked the statement "I feel bad about myself if my house is not perfect," you are falling into this trap.

The final characteristic of a perfectionist is lowered self-esteem.

Lowered Self-Esteem

If a perfectionist thinks in either-or terminology ("Everything I do is either good or bad") and if a perfectionist sets unrealistic goals for herself ("I must always be perfect at my job"), she is setting herself up for lowered self-esteem. Nobody, positively nobody, is that perfect—except God. If you checked "I expect the best of myself," you may have fallen into this trap.

How can we perfectionists crawl out of this pit?

Hope for the Perfectionist

As David Stoop says in his book, the battleground in this war is the mind. We need to change our way of thinking. Proverbs 23:7 says, "For as he thinks in his heart, so is he."

I particularly like three of the practical ways Stoop suggests in his book:

1. Reset Our Personal Goals

Dr. Stoop suggests that we perfectionists shift our thinking from setting personal goals to trying to define our life purpose. "Why am I here on earth?" "How do I want to be remembered after I'm dead and gone?"

Take a moment to answer those two questions:

I am here on earth to . . .

The Christian answer to this question is obviously to become like Christ. (But don't be caught by perfectionism here. We are trying to become like Him; we will never completely succeed until we are with Him in heaven.) You might also have another answer too.

I want to be remembered as . . .

You might answer "a good mother or wife," but don't employ either-or thinking here. A good mother or wife is not a perfect mother or wife—just someone who is trying.

Once we know the answers to these two questions, we can set sub-goals, realistic steps that will accomplish these overall goals. Stoop even suggests that one of our goals might be something we have avoided for fear of failure. We might challenge ourselves to see how long it actually takes to achieve a realistic goal in this area. (Remember the wife who wouldn't learn to play golf? That wife could set her goal: just to be able to hit the ball well enough to play without holding others back. And she might take lessons and start playing with a girlfriend who is more interested in enjoying the game than being good.)

Set one or two sub-goals under the heading "I am here on earth." (Remember, don't set too many goals—and be realistic. Your overall sub-goal might be to grow in your faith, to serve God, or to be a friend to someone who is hurting.)

Then set one or two sub-goals under the heading "I want to be remembered as." (A sub-goal might be: I want to be remembered as someone who spent a lot of time helping others.)

2. Enjoy a Personal Treat

Perfectionists are often so busy trying to be perfect that they spend little time relaxing or enjoying life. Having lunch with a friend might seem to be a waste of time and money, yet some recreation is needed. A vacation might also seem to be too costly. But it also is important.

Write down the special treat you plan for yourself in the space below:

Now set a specific time when you will do this:

3. Work on Thought Patterns

That's what we are doing throughout this pitfall section. As you read the Scriptures at the end of each pitfall, you are replacing old thought patterns with truths from the Bible. Read through the Scriptures at the end of this pitfall. Then determine to memorize one a week for the next month.

Also take three areas in which you are a perfectionist and analyze the process involved in the diagram on the following page. I will demonstrate one, then you fill in three others.

The apostle Paul, the greatest evangelist of all time, did not think he was perfect. He said, "Not that I have already attained, or am already perfected; but I press on, that I may lay hold of that for which Christ Jesus has also laid hold of me" (Phil. 3:12).

He also acknowledged his struggle to do what was right: "For what I am doing, I do not understand. For what I will to do, that I do not practice; but what I hate, that I do . . . For I know that in me (that is, in my flesh) nothing good dwells" (Rom. 7:15,18).

If the apostle Paul, who gave his life for Christ, knew he was not perfect, why do we think we are—or should be?

True Perfection

God says He wants to make you something more than your human excellence can ever be. He wants to love you into wholeness. You will rise to the level and degree that you sense His love in your life. That's why I no longer worry about being perfect because the perfection of Christ is manifested by His love flowing through me.

When you look in the mirror and see the excellence of Jesus reflected back, that's when you will have a sense of your true worth. The actual transformation takes place every time you worship the Lord for *His* perfection. Never forget Paul's admonition to the Hebrew Christians: "For the law made nothing perfect" (Heb. 7:19 NIV); and realize that your striving will make nothing perfect.

When This Happens	I Think . . .	And Do . . .	Instead I Will Think . . .
I have not been able to put my house in an attractive order.	I fear that if people see it, they will think poorly of me.	As a result, I don't ever have people over or show hospitality.	God has provided me with a home. I will be grateful for what I have and stop judging my home. I will focus on how I can use it to show hospitality to others.

Scriptures to Consider When You Are Trying to Combat Perfectionism

For by grace you have been saved through faith, and that not of yourselves; it is the gift of God, not of works, lest anyone should boast. For we are His workmanship, created in Christ Jesus for good works. (Ephesians 2:4–5, 8–10)

For all have sinned and fall short of the glory of God, being justified freely by His grace through the redemption that is in Christ Jesus . . . Where is the boasting then? It is excluded. By what law? Of works? No, but by the law of faith. Therefore we conclude that a man is justified by faith apart from the deeds of the law. (Romans 3:23–24,27–28)

There is none righteous, no, not one;
There is none who understands . . .
They have all turned aside;
They have together become unprofitable;
There is none who does good, no, not one.
(Romans 3:10–12)

Then, when desire has conceived, it gives birth to sin; and sin, when it is full-grown, brings forth death. Do not be deceived, my beloved brethren. Every good gift and every perfect gift is from above, and comes down from the Father of lights, with whom there is no variation or shadow of turning. (James 1:15–17)

THE PITFALL OF PRIDE

THE LIE: *"I'm in control of my life, and I can make things happen the
way I want them to happen."*

I always believed I didn't have pride. In fact, I took pride in that! But it
wasn't true. When I was working as a television entertainer, I feared failure even more than I desired success. This fear of failure was not humility, but pride. I felt I deserved to be successful. But my pride made me all
the more susceptible to failure.

The deception of pride is thinking that our will is more important than
God's will. This was Satan's downfall. He didn't want to let God be God
and do things His way. Satan's last words before he was cast out of heaven
were these: "I will exalt my throne above the stars of God" (Isa. 14:13).
Satan was perfect before pride took root in his heart and he decided that
God's will was no longer as important as his own. Pride is a conceited
sense of one's superiority.

Pride can also be a mask for fear.

A Mask for Fear

Sometimes pride comes from being afraid you have no value as a person.
It says, "I have to be great because I fear I'll be nothing." At the opposite
extreme is the thought, *If I can't be the best, then I'll be the worst. If I can't
make people love me, then I'll make them hate me.* Prisons are crowded with
people who have felt this way.

The more spiritually mature we become, the more we see that without
God we are nothing. It is He who gives us our worth: "For if anyone thinks
himself to be something, when he is nothing, he deceives himself" (Gal. 6:3).

Other times pride comes from arrogance. King Nebuchadnezzar's life is a biblical case study in pride and its consequences. If you are tempted by pride—and most of us are—then watch as God deals with this sin in Nebuchadnezzar's life.

Most of us know the story of Shadrach, Meshach, and Abednego, the three young Hebrew boys who were thrown into the fiery furnace. Who put them there? Our friend Nebuchadnezzar did, because they would not worship a golden statue. Many believe this statute depicted the king himself. It was a golden image ninety feet tall, built on a flat, expansive land to make it seem even larger—and to allow multitudes to gather around and worship it. What an example of pride to the extreme.

And when the Hebrew boys refused to bow down to this statue, Nebuchadnezzar decided to take their lives.

But God saved the boys—and even comforted them in the fiery furnace. The king saw four images walking around that blazing inferno, none of whom were burned by the heat.

Even Nebuchadnezzar had to admit that their God was greater than his pagan gods.

Yet the king continued in his pride. When he described his dream in Daniel 4, he revealed how centered he was upon himself: "*I*, Nebuchadnezzar, was at rest in *my* house, and flourishing in *my* palace. *I* saw a dream which made *me* afraid, and the thoughts on *my* bed and the visions of *my* head troubled *me*. Therefore *I* issued a decree to bring in all the wise men of Babylon before *me*, that they might make known to *me* the interpretation of the dream (Dan. 4:4–6, emphasis added). Nebuchadnezzar uses the word *I*, and the possessive of this first-person pronoun, nineteen times in verses 4 through 10. Self-centered? Yes. Prideful? Very.

And his dream predicted God's judgment of his pride: "let him graze with the beasts of the field, till seven times pass over him" (Dan. 4:23).

At first this prophecy seemed delayed. And the prophet Daniel told the king he might delay God's judgment. "Break off your sins by being righteous, and your iniquities by showing mercy to the poor" (Dan. 4:27).

But the king didn't listen. A year later he is roaming through his palace, muttering to himself, "Is not this great Babylon, that I have built for a royal dwelling by my mighty power and for the honor of my majesty?" (Dan.

4:30). Me, me, me. Mine, mine, mine. Sounds like a toddler who believes that everything around him is his.

Right then, God speaks and executes his judgment. For the next seven years this great, prideful king lived as an animal in the field, overcome by mental illness.

But Nebuchadnezzar did not remain there. He finally lifted his eyes to heaven and saw God for who He is. "For His dominion is an everlasting dominion, / And His kingdom is from generation to generation" (Dan 4:34). And the proud king finally sees himself for who he is: a flawed mortal. He says, "All the inhabitants of the earth are reputed as nothing; He [God] does according to His will in the army of heaven and among the inhabitants of the earth" (Dan 4:35).

The great king Nebuchadnezzar said finally, "Now I, Nebuchadnezzar, praise and extol and honor the King of heaven, all of whose works are truth, and His ways justice. And those who walk in pride He is able to put down" (Dan. 4:36–37).

Nebuchadnezzar reigned as king of Babylon for many years after his sanity returned. Altogether he ruled the country for forty-three years, building the world-famous hanging gardens.

When I'm tempted by pride, I try to remember Nebuchadnezzar's testimony. I praise and honor the King of heaven. And I never forget that God will abase those who walk in pride.

How about you? Do you tend to think, *I'm in control of my life, and I can make things happen the way I want them to happen*?

Before you answer no, take a quick inventory of your own life by checking the statements below that apply to you:

_____ "I like to show other people my accomplishments."

_____ "I tend to think I am quicker and smarter than others."

_____ "I don't need help from anyone."

_____ "I have come a long way, and I intend to go even further."

When you are tempted to think this way, consider how you would like to be seen in God's eyes.

Here's one description that is available to all who are prideful: "Pride serves as their necklace; Violence covers them like a garment. Their eyes bulge with abundance . . . They scoff and speak wickedly concerning oppression" (Ps. 73:6–8). That's how God sees people who fall into the pit of pride.

Or would you prefer this second option: "Seek the LORD, all you meek of the earth, / who have upheld His justice . . . It may be that you will be hidden / In the day of the LORD's anger" (Zeph. 2:3). That's how God sees the humble of heart.

It takes a lot of healing to come from feeling like a nothing to accepting your worth in Jesus, then to admitting that apart from God you are nothing. But when you can do that, it will be God in you that leads you to greatness. Ask God to give you a humble heart. He will.

Scriptures to Consider When You Are Trying to Combat Pride

Pride goes before destruction,
And a haughty spirit before a fall.
Better to be of a humble spirit with the lowly,
Than to divide the spoil with the proud.
(Proverbs 16:18–19)

A man's pride will bring him low,
But the humble in spirit will retain honor. (Proverbs 29:23)

The wicked in his pride persecutes the poor;
Let them be caught in the plots which they have devised.
(Psalm 10:2)

There they cry out, but He does not answer,
Because of the pride of evil men. (Job 35:12)

Therefore pride serves as their necklace;
Violence covers them like a garment.
Their eyes bulge with abundance;
They have more than heart could wish.
They scoff and speak wickedly concerning oppression;
They speak loftily,
They set their mouth against the heavens,
And their tongue walks through the earth. (Psalm 73:6–9)

When pride comes, then comes shame;
But with the humble is wisdom. (Proverbs 11:2)

The wicked in his proud countenance does not seek God;
God is in none of his thoughts. (Psalm 10:4)

The Pitfall of Rebellion

THE LIE: *"I think this is right for me, so I'm going to do it, no matter what God or anyone else says."*

A number of years ago I had corrective surgery for an old childhood injury. The doctor's instructions were "Stay home for two months and do no lifting, no bending, no walking, no exercising, no quick movements, and no straining." In other words, no life.

For the first couple of weeks, I was too groggy to read the Bible very much or do any in-depth praying, so I watched a lot of television and looked through many secular magazines. Once my convalescence ended, I slowly made efforts to get back into my normal routine.

But things were different. I didn't read the Bible as much, and I was too busy for the prayer closet, opting rather to pray and run. Slowly I began to make decisions for my life without asking God. I began walking in rebellion by serving my own needs. Unfortunately, I didn't realize I had drifted away from God until the fruit of my decisions proved that I had.

Do you recognize any of the following signs in your life that indicate you are moving toward rebelliousness?

_____ "I make all decisions on my own without asking God for wisdom."

_____ "I don't attend Bible studies because I feel I know all there is to know."

_____ "I don't have time for prayer and Bible reading because I'm too busy."

_____ "I am afraid of giving money to the church and to the poor, because I might need this money for myself."

_____ "I often don't attend church because I have more important things to do with that time."

If you checked any of the statements above, you are falling into spiritual apathy, which is the foundation of rebellion.

Unfortunately, we often rationalize spiritual apathy and call it spiritual maturity. The statements "I've attended a Bible study for years; I know all there is to know so I've decided to quit" and " I really haven't had much time for prayer and Bible study lately; I'm just too busy" show misguided thinking. Because all of us are susceptible to spiritual apathy, "we must give the more earnest heed to the things we have heard, lest we drift away" (Heb. 2:1).

If you engage in activity that you know is not right, you have bought into the lie that says, "I think this is right for me, so I'm going to do it, no matter what God or anyone else says." The deception of rebellion is in thinking that our way is better than God's. *Rebellion is pride put into action.*

The Bible says, "Rebellion is as the sin of witchcraft" (1 Sam. 15:23). Witchcraft is, of course, total opposition to God. The same verse says that stubbornness is idolatry. Pride *puts* us in rebellion. Stubbornness *keeps* us in rebellion. *There is an idol in the life of anyone who walks stubbornly in rebellion. Identifying and smashing that idol is the key to coming back into alignment with God.*

The Chief Rebel

The rebel of all rebels is Satan. Pride definitely put this former angel into rebellion. Isaiah describes Lucifer's fall in this way:

> For you have said in your heart:
> "I will ascend into heaven,
> I will exalt my throne above the stars of God . . .
> I will ascend above the heights of the clouds,
> I will be like the Most High." (Isa. 14:13–14)

And what is Satan's punishment for rebelling against God? He will be bound in a bottomless pit for a thousand years, then released for a short while, and finally cast into the lake of fire and brimstone where he will be tormented day and night forever and ever (Rev. 20:2–3,10).

What happens to those who fall into the pitfall of rebellion? God is very clear about this throughout Scripture. The prophet Nehemiah tells us the outcome of the rebels in his generation: "Nevertheless they were disobedient and rebelled against You . . . Therefore You delivered them into the hand of their enemies, who oppressed them" (Neh. 9:26–27).

Satan was cast out of heaven and now roams the earth, enticing men to follow him in rebellion. Actually he's been quite successful over the last centuries. Even the Israelites, God's chosen people, have rebelled against God—over and over again.

The Israelites' walk in rebellion can be an example for us—and for what will happen to us if we rebel against God's commandments. The prophet Jeremiah tells part of this story in Lamentations.

Here we see Jeremiah, often called the "weeping prophet," expressing his grief that the Israelites have rejected God—the God who made them, loved them, and stood beside them. And God judges them for their disobedience. Jerusalem, their capital city, has fallen to the Babylonians, and the people are being carried into captivity. Jeremiah stands in the middle of the rubble and describes what he sees:

"Jerusalem . . . has been tossed away like a filthy rag," the prophet says. "All who once honored her now despise her, for they have seen her stripped naked and humiliated" (Lam. 1:8 NLT). Jeremiah is describing the plight of the Jewish people, but this applies to us as well if we rebel against God.

And Jeremiah goes on to describe how God has removed Himself from His people. "You have covered Yourself with a cloud *that prayer should not pass through*" (Lam. 3:44, emphasis added).

Are you willing to have God reject your prayers? Think about what that could mean to you in the future.

Jeremiah tells us what happened to the Israelites:

Our inheritance has been turned over to strangers, our homes to foreigners . . . Those who pursue us are at our heels; we are exhausted but are given no rest . . . We must hunt for food in the wilderness at the risk of our lives. Because of the famine, our skin has been blackened as though baked in an oven . . . Our hearts are sick and weary, and our eyes grow dim with tears. (Lam. 5:2,5,9–10, 17–15 NLT)

How did people rebel to deserve such punishment?

For one thing, they looked to their neighbors, the Egyptians, to help them—rather than looking to God for help. (Interesting that they would look to Egypt for help. What short memories they must have had. Their forefathers had run from this country because the Egyptians had enslaved them.)

Have you tended to rely on your own resources and the resources of friends for help, rather than God?

Are you listening to God's Word? Are you obeying it? Obedience is a sure sign of your love for God.

Jeremiah's remedy for the plight of the Israelites stands also for us today. He says:

> Arise, cry out in the night,
> At the beginning of the watches;
> Pour out your heart like water before the face of the Lord.
> Lift your hands toward Him. (Lam. 2:19)

Are you willing to take the steps Jeremiah outlines here? If so, write a prayer in the space below asking God to keep you from falling into rebellion.

Are you also willing to "lift your hands toward Him" in worship and praise? If so, write a prayer of praise to God here.

Hear God speak this promise directly to you by inserting your name in the blanks:

> If you, _____, are willing and obedient,
> You shall eat the good of the land;
> But if you refuse and rebel,
> You, _____, shall be devoured by the sword.
> (Isa. 1:19–20)

And what can you expect of God for walking with Him? The same response that Jeremiah expected: mercy. Jeremiah says:

> Through the LORD's mercies we are not consumed,
> Because His compassions fail not.
> They are new every morning;
> Great is Your faithfulness.
> "The LORD is my portion," says my soul,
> "Therefore I hope in Him!" (Lam. 3:22–24)

In the midst of the rubble, the hunger, the enslavement of his people, Jeremiah still knows that God has a hopeful future for His repentant people. And He has the same hope for us.

Centuries later Thomas O. Chisholm and William M. Runyan wrote the hymn "Great Is Thy Faithfulness" to testify to God's mercy in their lives. They ended the hymn with these assurances:

> Pardon for sin and a peace that endureth,
> Thine own dear presence to cheer and to guide,
> Strength for today and bright hope for tomorrow.
> Blessings all mine, with ten thousand beside![1]

That's the promise God makes to us if we turn from our rebellion and walk back into His arms.

Scripture to Consider When You Are Trying to Overcome Rebellion

"Nevertheless they were disobedient
And rebelled against You,
Cast Your law behind their backs . . .
Therefore You delivered them into the hand of their enemies,
Who oppressed them." (Nehemiah 9:26–27)

I will mention the lovingkindnesses of the LORD . . .
And the great goodness toward the house of Israel,
Which He has bestowed on them according to His mercies . . .
But they rebelled and grieved His Holy Spirit;
So He turned Himself against them as an enemy,
And He fought against them. (Isaiah 63:7,10)

30

THE PITFALL OF REJECTION

THE LIE: *"I'm not worth anything, so it's completely understandable that people will reject me."*

My earliest memory of rejection is of my mother locking me in a closet. Had it been an isolated incident, it might not have been so bad. But it wasn't. It happened countless times. As a result, I grew up feeling rejected, and the feelings of rejection grew in me until no amount of affirmation and encouragement could overcome them.

This is the lie we believe when we feel rejection: "I'm not worth anything, so it's completely understandable that people will reject me." A spirit of rejection convinces you that you will be rejected, and then every word and action of other people is interpreted through the eyes of rejection.

Each of us has been rejected—by a family member, a friend, a teacher, a stranger, or a casual acquaintance. Michael's long working hours, the moments he was short with me—I saw each of them as rejection. When he and I went to a marriage counselor, the counselor said, "You've allowed a spirit of rejection to color everything you've heard each other say.

"Rejection is a spirit that has to be fed to stay alive," the counselor continued, "and it has to be starved in order to kill it. It is fed and grows by believing negative thoughts about yourself. It is starved to death by refusing to give it the destructive food it wants and instead building and nourishing yourself on the love and acceptance of God."

How about you? Have you interpreted other people's actions as rejection? Think through your relationships with the following people and mention the moments you might have misinterpreted a situation:

Your husband, wife, girlfriend, or boyfriend:

A family member:

A friend:

Now think about those situations. What negative thoughts about yourself could have made you misinterpret these moments?

With your husband, wife, girlfriend, or boyfriend:

With a family member:

With a friend:

The counselor told Michael and me, "It's not that the power of this spirit of rejection is greater than the Lord's power to cast it out, but you can't be delivered from something you are giving place to. If you feed a stray dog, he's going to stay. If you are feeding a spirit of rejection, it's going to stay also. The best way to starve a spirit of rejection is to fill yourself with the knowledge of God's acceptance."

This counselor sent us home with the assignment to find all the verses in the Bible about God's acceptance. And that's my assignment for you now, except that I have already found the Scriptures for you. Look up the following verses, and write them in the blank spaces:

God has chosen you . . .

Deuteronomy 7:6

2 Thessalonians 2:13–17

Isaiah 43:10

Acts 22:14

1 Peter 2:9

And Scripture makes it very clear that once God has chosen you, He will not reject you . . .

Psalm 94:14

1 Samuel 12:22

You are accepted by the living God. You should not feel rejection or sense it from other people. Hear the Lord speaking to you as you write your name in this passage of Scripture:

> I have chosen you, _____ and have not cast you away:
> Fear not, I am with you, _____; be not dismayed,
> For I am your God. I will strengthen you,
> Yes, I will help you,
> I will uphold you with My righteous right hand. (Isa. 41:9-10)

By the time Michael and I had compiled our long list and been through six weeks of talking to this counselor, our relationship was renewed, and each of us found healing in our own souls.

Living Like a Chosen One

God said, "I chose you out of the world" (John 15:19). We did not choose Jesus first; He chose us. We must learn to live like the chosen ones we are.

When you sense the red light of rejection flashing off and on in your brain over some word or action someone has said or done, remember that Jesus chose *you*. Remember, too, that *the voice of God always encourages; the voice of the devil always discourages*. If you can't see anything good about yourself, it's because the devil has covered up your future with your past.

Every time you feel rejection in any way, refuse to accept it. Say, "Spirit of rejection, I reject you! God accepts me and loves me just the way I am. I have been chosen by God, and I choose to live in His full acceptance."

Finally, write a prayer in the space below, thanking God for loving you and asking Him to help you rebuke the spirit of rejection.

Scriptures to Consider When You Are Attacked by a Spirit of Rejection

These verses clearly show God's love for you.

And He will love you and bless you and multiply you.
(Deuteronomy 7:13)

I love those who love me. (Proverbs 8:17)

"Yes, I have loved you with an everlasting love:
Therefore with lovingkindness I have drawn you."
(Jeremiah 31:3)

"As the Father loved Me, I also have loved you; abide in My love." (Jesus' words in John 15:9–10)

Who shall separate us from the love of Christ? Shall tribulation, or distress, or persecution, or famine, or nakedness, or peril, or sword . . . Yet in all these things we are more than conquerors through Him who loved us.
(Romans 8:35,37)

But God, who is rich in mercy, because of His great love with which He loved us, even when we were dead in trespasses, made us alive together with Christ (by grace you have been saved), and raised us up together, and made us sit together in the heavenly places in Christ Jesus.
(Ephesians 2:4–6)

31

THE PITFALL OF SELF-PITY

THE LIE: *"The worst things always happen to me. Good things seldom come my way."*

People who have been emotionally damaged early in life often end up negatively self-focused. The lie that plays over and over in their minds is: "The worst things always happen to me. Good things seldom come my way." When you rehearse misery day after day, you open yourself up to an evil spirit. Allowing yourself to feel sorry for yourself all the time means you are ignoring the power of God in your life now. And that's exactly what Satan wants. Self-pity forever keeps you from moving into all God has for you.

Think about your own life. Do you ever feel sorry for yourself? List those moments below:

Looking at that list, do you believe you have legitimate reasons for feeling this way? Explain below.

Write a prayer asking God to set you free from all self-pity. Tell Him how grateful you are that you don't ever have to feel sorry for yourself, because you are His child and He has great things ahead for your future. Tell Him all the things you are thankful for in your life.

Now look again at the reasons for your feeling of self-pity. Are they as significant in the light of God's blessings to you—and His continual care? Scripture says, "And the LORD, He is the One who goes before you. He will be with you, He will not leave you nor forsake you; do not fear nor be dismayed" (Deut. 31:8).

Jesus had plenty of reason to wallow in self-pity. One of the greatest was His mission to die on the cross for our sins. When He tells the disciples of His destiny, Peter reacts by rebuking the Lord. "Far be it from You, Lord," he says. "This shall not happen to You!"

But Jesus will not allow Himself to be filled with sorrow or self-pity. He turns to Peter and says, "Get behind Me, Satan! You are an offense to Me, for you are not mindful of the things of God, but the things of men" (Matt. 16:23).

I admit that we can't be entirely like Jesus, but we can try. And Jesus rejected self-pity as sinful, as the lure of Satan. Instead, He told us to turn our focus toward God.

Focus on God

Self-pity keeps us focused entirely inward. We mistakenly think that an intense focus on ourselves will contribute most to our happiness and fulfillment, when actually the opposite is true. Dwelling on ourselves leads to emotional sickness. Instead of being filled with thoughts about what we need and feel, we must be full of thoughts of the Lord.

Our complete focus must be on God alone. The Bible says, "The backslider in heart will be filled with his own ways, / But a good man will be satisfied from above" (Prov. 14:14). In his classic devotional *My Utmost for His Highest,* Oswald Chambers says, "No sin is worse than the sin of self-pity, because it removes God from the throne of our lives, replacing Him with our own self-interests. It causes us to open our mouths only to complain, and we simply become spiritual sponges—always absorbing, never giving, and never being satisfied. And there is nothing lovely or generous about our lives."[1]

Ask yourself, what would have to happen for your day to be a good one? List those things below. Then thank God that this is the day He has made, and you will rejoice and be glad in it.

Oswald Chambers says, "The Sermon on the Mount indicates that when we are on a mission for Jesus Christ, there is no time to stand up for ourselves. Jesus says, in effect, 'Don't worry about whether or not you are being treated justly.' Looking for justice is actually a sign that we have been diverted from our devotion to Him. Never look for justice in this world, but never cease to give it. If we look for justice, we will only begin to complain and to indulge ourselves in the discontent of self-pity, as if to say, 'Why should I be treated like this?' If we are devoted to Jesus Christ, we have nothing to do with what we encounter, whether it is just or unjust. In essence, Jesus says, 'Continue steadily on with what I have told you to do, and I will guard your life. If you try to guard it yourself, you remove yourself from My deliverance.' Even the most devout among us become atheistic in this regard—we do not believe Him. We put our common sense on the throne and then attach God's name to it. We do lean to our own understanding, instead of trusting God will all our hearts."[2]

Resolve now that you will no longer allow self-pity to be a part of your life. Say aloud, "I refuse to sit around thinking about what I need and want and feel. I refuse to mourn and complain about the past, present, and future. I deliberately choose to think about only You, Lord, and Your goodness. I look to You to meet all my needs. You know what they are even better than I do."

After Peter objected to the Lord's sacrifice on Calvary, Jesus told His disciples, "If anyone desires to come after Me, let him deny himself, and take up his cross, and follow Me. For whoever desires to save his life will lose it, but whoever loses his life for My sake will find it. For what profit is it to a man if he gains the whole world, and loses his own soul?" (Matt. 16:24–26).

This is the Christian life. To take up *our own cross* and follow Him. There's no room for self-pity here. Only obedience and faith.

Scriptures to Consider as You
Look to Overcome Self-Pity

Whoever has no rule over his own spirit
Is like a city broken down, without walls. (Proverbs 25:28)

I have been crucified with Christ; it is no longer I who live, but Christ lives in me; and the life which I now live in the flesh I live by faith in the Son of God, who loved me and gave Himself for me. (Galatians 2:20)

For godly sorrow produces repentance leading to salvation, not to be regretted; but the sorrow of the world produces death. (2 Corinthians 7:10)

But you, beloved, building yourselves up on your most holy faith, praying in the Holy Spirit, keep yourselves in the love of God, looking for the mercy of our Lord Jesus Christ unto eternal life. (Jude 20–21)

THE PITFALL OF SUICIDE

THE FIRST LIE: *"There is no way out."*
THE SECOND LIE: *"Therefore death is the only means of escape."*

One night when I was fourteen, my mother unleashed a venomous verbal attack, accusing me of things I had not done. I was helpless to defend myself against her rage, and I suffered such extreme loneliness, depression, and hopelessness that I felt crushed emotionally. I saw no possibility for things to ever be any different, and I decided I didn't want to live. I took an overdose of drugs that night, but it was not to attract attention or make people feel sorry for me. I simply did not want to wake up again.

At that age I accepted the lie that there is no way out, and therefore death is the only means of escape.

Nearly everyone with any serious emotional damage will consider suicide at one time or another. If that ever happens to you, remember that those thoughts come from Satan.

Suicide is a sin. The commandment "You shall not kill" is not invalidated simply because the victim is yourself. Suicide is never God's will for you.

The apostle Paul told the Corinthians: "Do you not know that your body is the temple of the Holy Spirit who is in you, whom you have from God, and you are not your own? For you were bought at a price; therefore glorify God in your body and in your spirit, which are God's" (1 Cor. 6:19–20).

God's will for you is to connect with His Spirit within you, not to destroy that Spirit and your body.

I know that many people think of suicide as selfish—and it is the final act of a person focused intently upon self—but I know from experience that when you're suicidal, something beyond selfishness overtakes you. I know that down deep you really want to live, but you don't want to live the way you've been living.

Fortunately, I didn't take enough drugs to do the job when I was fourteen, so I ended up sick instead of dead. When I did wake up, however, I felt different, even though nothing in my circumstances had changed. I wasn't sure why I had been spared from death, but somehow I didn't feel like dying anymore. I felt like fighting back, and I decided to do it by taking steps to get out of my miserable situation.

That's why it's important to remember, even in the midst of suicidal thoughts, that at any moment in our lives, things can change. In fact, change is inevitable. The only thing that doesn't change is God: "For I am the LORD, I do not change" (Mal. 3:6). God is always working on your behalf. You may feel like killing yourself now, but tomorrow afternoon you could feel entirely different.

Resisting Thoughts of Suicide

The pain that produces suicidal impulses can arise from a number of sources.

People in the Bible also experienced this pain. Check the thoughts below that apply to you:

_____ "Therefore I hated life because the work that was done
under the sun was distressing to me, for all is vanity and
grasping for the wind." (Solomon in Eccl. 2:17)

_____ "For the thing I greatly feared has come upon me,
And what I dreaded has happened to me.
I am not at ease, nor am I quiet;
I have no rest, for trouble comes." (Job in Job 3:25–26)

_____ "What strength do I have, that I should hope?
And what is my end, that I should prolong my life? . . .
Is my help not within me?
And is success driven from me?" (Job 6:11,13)

_____ "So I have been allotted months of futility,
And wearisome nights have been appointed to me.
When I lie down, I say, 'When shall I arise,
And the night be ended?'
For I have had my fill of tossing till dawn." (Job 7:3–4)

Neither of these men—King Solomon nor Job—committed suicide, but they certainly thought about it.

Whether you feel suicidal at this moment or not, you need to confess before the Lord any time in your life that you ever said or thought that you wanted to die. Write that prayer in the space below.

Now write another prayer that asserts Satan's position in your current thoughts. (Be sure to renounce Satan in Jesus' name and reject his lying spirit. Smash the spirit of suicide and refuse any voice that says you deserve it. Then assert that your future is not hopeless, that you want to live and glorify your Father God.)

Say this prayer aloud. If you have to say it twenty times a day, do it.

I was freed from a spirit of suicide in the counseling office with Mary Anne, so I was never gripped by it again. However, several times since that spirit has taunted me. When I prayed, those thoughts left. Remember Paul's insight to Timothy: "And the Lord will deliver me from every evil work and preserve me for His heavenly kingdom" (2 Tim. 4:18).

Once you renounce wanting to die, you will have to deal with why you wanted to die in the first place. Check the statements below that might apply to you:

_____ "I have a physical illness that I'm afraid I won't recover from."

_____ "I am ashamed of what I have done and cannot live with the guilt."

_____ "I am so lonely. I have no friends and few acquaintances. No one really cares about me."

_____ "I am losing my battle with alcohol (or drugs)."

_____ "I feel crazy at times. My mother (father) was mentally ill. I fear I might have inherited it."

_____ "A loved one has recently died. I feel I have nothing to live for."

_____ "I have just experienced a divorce. I feel overwhelmed by life."

_____ "I was physically (or sexually) abused as a child and I can't seem to get over the pain."

_____ "I have experienced a major financial loss."

_____ "I have lost my job and fear I won't ever find another one."

_____ "I have been depressed for some time and have been unable to get over it."

Now that you have some idea of what is bothering you, you need to get help. Seek out someone who can counsel you. A Christian psychologist would be best, but you can also call a suicide hotline, a psychiatrist, a pastor, a counselor, or a strong believer in the Lord.

As you do so, think about Job's life. He is the man who had everything in the Bible: money, power, respect, health, a loving family. Yet all of a sudden what he dreaded most happened to him. He lost his health, his sons and daughters, and his wealth. His wife even suggested that he commit suicide.

And Job's thoughts continually turned in that way. He said, "My soul loathes my life" (Job 10:1). The entire fourteenth chapter of the book of Job is an elegy on death.

Job wanted God to answer the question we all ask, "Why has this happened to me?" He longed for someone to intercede for him. "God is not mortal like me, so I cannot argue with him or take him to trial. If only there were a mediator who could bring us together, but there is none . . . Then I could speak to him without fear, but I cannot do that in my own strength" (Job 9:32–33,35 NLT).

Job was looking for a mediator—and we have one. Jesus Christ. A Man we can talk to because He became one of us and understands our pain.

Have you ever felt that death would be better than the life you are living? If so, write out a prayer confessing those thoughts to God and ask Him to set you free from them.

And then hear Him speak back to you:

For I know the thoughts that I think toward you, _____, says the LORD, thoughts of peace and not of evil, to give you a future and a hope. (Jer. 29:11)

Even in the midst of Job's blaming God, he was able to say, "Though He slay me, yet will I trust Him" (Job 13:15).

That is the reason Job never committed suicide. Through all his difficulty, he still trusted God. Later he verbalized his total faith in God: "For I know that my Redeemer lives, and He shall stand at last on the earth" (Job 19:25).

Are you able to put your trust in God right now? Are you willing to surrender your life to Him knowing He will do good things in you and in your circumstances?

The Best Is Yet to Come

Pastor Jack always taught us that the best part of our lives is ahead. In the more than thirty years I've walked with Jesus, this has proven true. That little girl who spent so much time locked in the closet now has a loving husband, three children who love the Lord, and a fulfilling and fruitful life. I never imagined these blessings, especially when I was contemplating suicide.

It doesn't matter whether or not you can see the possibility of a good future at the moment, God has great things in store for you. Jesus said, "I have come that they may have life, and that they may have it more abundantly" (John 10:10).

Hear Jesus saying to you:

And God is able to make all grace abound toward you, _____, that you, _____, always having all sufficiency in all things, may have an abundance for every good work. (2 Cor. 9:8)

Scriptures to Consider When You Are Thinking of Suicide

I waited patiently for the LORD;
And He inclined to me,
And heard my cry.
He also brought me up out of a horrible pit,
Out of the miry clay,
And set my feet upon a rock,
And established my steps.
He has put a new song in my mouth—
Praise to our God. (David's words in Psalm 40:1–3)

Concerning this thing I pleaded with the Lord three times that it might depart from me. And He said to me, "My grace is sufficient for you, for My strength is made perfect in weakness." Therefore most gladly I will rather boast in my infirmities, that the power of Christ may rest upon me. (2 Corinthians 12:8–9, Paul's words in reference to his thorn in the flesh)

Step 7
Stand Strong

Believe that as long as you stand with God
and don't give up, you win.

33

TRUSTING GOD FOR EVERY STEP

*I*f we are to have total deliverance, total wholeness, and total restoration, there comes a time when we have to stand up and say, "This is what I believe; this is the way I will live; this is what I will and will not accept—and that's the way it is."

One of the last times I saw Mary Anne before she moved away, I went to her for some problem I don't even remember now. What I do remember was her wise counsel, which amounted to two words: "Grow up," she said lovingly.

"What?" I asked.

"It's time to grow up, Stormie," she repeated in her patient voice. When my mother screamed those words at me for years, it felt like a beating. When Mary Anne said them, it felt like the Holy Spirit.

"Stormie, you need to get alone with the Lord and ask Him the questions you're asking me. Then you tell me what He's saying to you."

I did ask the Lord, just as Mary Anne said, and I did hear the answer, just as she predicted. It was then I knew without a doubt that I had everything I needed for my life right within me. I just had to stand strong in the Lord. I walked a little taller after that.

Your Personal Spiritual History

In his book *Regaining the Power of Youth*, Dr. Kenneth Cooper mentions the health benefits of a personal spiritual walk. He cites numerous studies, one of which was conducted by Yale University. More than twenty-eight-hundred elderly subjects were followed over a twelve-year period. Participants who attended religious services regularly were "more likely to have better physical functional ability later in life," "more optimism," and "fewer symptoms of depression." In a Duke University study, those who regularly attended religious services displayed stronger immune systems than those who didn't attend.

These studies and other studies like them show that regular pursuit of religious disciplines increase the likelihood that a person remains vigorous and healthy well into old age.[1]

Cooper suggests that his readers take their own personal spiritual histories, much as doctors take a physical history when they examine a new patient. And Cooper says that some doctors have also begun taking a patient's spiritual history, which will help them predict "the impact of that person's spirituality on preventing disease, healing, or coping with the pain and discomfort of chronic illness."[2]

I'd like to suggest that you write up your own spiritual history as you determine to stand strong in the days ahead. Cooper has readers assess their spiritual walks in five different areas:

1. *The point or period when the spiritual dimension became important.* Include dates, your feelings, and other people who were involved.

Moment	Date	Your Feelings	Others

Now describe the specific changes that have occurred since then:

In Your Inner Life	Your Moral Views	Your Social Interactions

2. *The major milestones in your spiritual journey.* Include special insights, spiritual breakthroughs, and renewal experiences.

Milestone	Changes in Your Inner Life	Changes in Outward Practices

3. *Situations in which your faith has made a difference in your health, energy, and emotional well-being:*

4. *What you believe about the outer limits of faith-based healing or health enhancements*—even if you haven't experienced or witnessed these phenomena. For instance, do you believe in miracles?

5. *Details of spiritual disciplines or practices you currently observe*—and the difference they have made in your life. For instance, Sunday or Wednesday night attendance at service, personal prayer, Bible or theological studies, healing services, volunteer work, service to the needy, and small group prayer or Bible Study meetings:

Spiritual Discipline	Difference in Your Life

Once you've completed your spiritual history, you should be able to see where you've made progress and where you still need improvement in your Christian walk as you stand strong in the days ahead.

Finally, establish some guidelines for the future. This is the time to stand up and say, "This is what I believe; this is the way I will live; this is what I will and will not accept—and that's the way it is."

Take a moment to state these beliefs. Write your thoughts in the space below:

This is what I believe:

This is the way I will live:

This is what I will accept:

This is what I will not accept:

—and that's the way it is.

If you've had some trouble working through this personal statement of faith, look up the Scriptures at the end of this chapter for reference, then go back and fill in any new thoughts.

We come to a point in our walk with the Lord when we've had enough teaching, enough counseling, enough deliverance, and enough knowledge of God's ways to be able to stand on our own two feet and say, "I am not going to live on the negative side of life any more."

The Bible says, "Let the weak say, 'I am strong'" (Joel 3:10). This does not mean that you say, "I think I can" like the Little Engine That Could in the children's book. If you are willing to say, "This is it. I will stand strong in the days ahead," write your name in the vow below:

I, _____, will stand firm in the Lord. I will stand strong against the enemy. I will not complain and lament over what isn't. I will rejoice over what is and all that God is doing.

Scriptures to Consider As You
Endeavor to Stand Strong

Write the verses below the Scripture to determine what you believe and the way you will live. Then go back and add anything you need to the exercise in this chapter. Once you have determined what you believe and the way you will live, you can decide what you will accept and not accept in the days ahead.

This is what I believe:

John 3:16

Romans 3:10–12

Isaiah 64:6

John 5:24

Jeremiah 30:17

John 14:6

John 3:3

John 16:13

James 5:16

This is the way I will live:

Luke 6:37

2 Corinthians 13:5

1 Timothy 4:13,16

Psalm 51:12–13

1 John 2:15–17

Colossians 3:5–8

1 Corinthians 10:31

Proverbs 13:3

Deuteronomy 15:10

James 1:5–8

2 Timothy 1:7

Ephesians 4:26–27

Zechariah 8:17

3 John 4

Proverbs 12:22

Exodus 20:2–20

Standing Strong When the Enemy Attacks

*T*here will be times when you are doing everything you know to do and things are going well, and then suddenly depression will cloud your mind. Or unforgiveness will return in full force, or you'll have a problem in an area where you've found deliverance and healing. This probably means you are under an attack from the devil.

At those times you have to understand without a doubt that when you walk with Jesus, you never walk backward. God has made it clear in His Word that if we have our eyes on Him, we will go from glory to glory and strength to strength (Ps. 84:7).

To go backward, you would have to deliberately turn your back on God and walk in the other direction. As long as you are looking to Him, you are moving forward. It does not matter how it feels; that's the way it is.

I don't want to reduce everything to steps and formulas, but sometimes we need simple guidelines. Often Satan's attack can be of such magnitude that we can hardly see straight, let alone figure out clear direction for ourselves. With that in mind, I have four suggestions that will help you navigate those rough times.

Four Ways to Recognize an Enemy Attack

1. Know God well enough to understand His heart.

Make sure that your knowledge of the Lord and your desire for His presence is so strong that you won't give the devil any ground. Satan will always try to push your back to the wall, but don't let him. Push his back to the wall by saying, "I will not allow defeat! My God is my defender and I refuse you entry into my life."

Get clear in your mind the things that are always true about God, and hold them alongside what is happening in your life to see if they line up.

- God loves me and nothing can separate me from His love (Rom. 8:37–39).

- God is merciful (Ex. 34:6–7).

- God is faithful (1 Cor. 1:8–9).

- God will forgive me (1 John 1:9).

- God will comfort me (Ps. 34:17–18).

- God will bless me (Rom. 10:12–13).

- God will guide me (Isa. 58:11).

- God is powerful (Isa. 14:27).

Say these truths about God over and over again when you are tempted by the devil. And write the actual Scripture verses in the space at the end of this chapter so you can speak these verses aloud when you are tempted by the devil.

2. *Know who Satan is.*

You may be thinking, I don't want any part of a battle with the devil. In fact, I prefer not to even think about things like that. Yet God and Satan are in a battle for your life. We must identify the enemy and the battle lines and make sure we're marching in the right army.

We worked through some Scriptures that identify the devil and his accomplices, demons, in chapter 11. Test your knowledge of who the devil is by filling in the blanks below:

Satan was _____. Now he roams _____.

Satan's sin was _____. His goal was _____.

Satan is _____. His goal now is _____.

But Satan is not all-powerful. In her book, *101 Things the Devil Can't Do*, Maisie Sparks shows us how limited Satan really is. For instance:

- *The Enemy can't win.* "But thanks be to God, who gives us the victory through our Lord Jesus Christ" (1 Cor. 15:57).[1]

- *The Adversary can't have you.* "Satan has asked for you, that he may sift you as wheat. But I have prayed for you, that your faith should not fail; and when you have returned to Me, strengthen your brethren" (Luke 22:31–32).[2]

- *The Critic can't make you feel guilty anymore.* "There is therefore now no condemnation to those who are in Christ Jesus, who do not walk according to the flesh, but according to the Spirit" (Rom. 8:1).[3]

One of Satan's plans is to keep people weighed down with guilt over things he is doing. He disguises himself as an angel, Scripture says, and sometimes even comes to you as you. At least you believe it's you. But it's not!

3. Know what makes you most susceptible to satanic attack.

Often we give Satan unintentional invitations to attack us by what we do or don't do. We can fend off much enemy attack by simply paying attention to the moments he gains access to our lives.

Think about your own life. At what moments are you tempted? List those moments below:

1.

2.

3.

4.

These are the times when you need to be particularly careful. Take a moment now and think about what you can do in the future to avoid these moments. List those ideas in the following spaces:

1.

2.

3.

4.

4. Know the signs of satanic attack.

If you learn to recognize the signs of satanic attack, you will be better able to establish your own defense and counterattack. If you don't, you may end up aiding the enemy. The devil can attack you through your mind, your emotions, your body, your relationships, or your circumstances. If you can immediately recognize negative emotions such as fear, guilt, depression, confusion, and lack of peace as coming from the enemy, instead of accepting them as truth, you can protect yourself better. Check the statements below to see if any of these seven signs of satanic attack are threatening you:

_____ "I experience sudden, paralyzing fear that leaves me incapacitated."

_____ "I have guilt that is overwhelming and doesn't respond to confession or a corrected walk."

_____ "I have recurring depression or depression that lasts a long time."

_____ "I have what feels like hell breaking loose in my mind, body, emotions, or situation, especially in an area where there has already been deliverance."

_____ "I have no peace about specific things that are happening to me."

_____ "I have great confusion at a point where I once had clarity."

_____ "I am receiving ideas in my mind that are in direct opposition to God's ways."

If you checked any of these statements, write a prayer below, asking God to stop this attack by Satan:

Praying with one or more believers about this is also very important.

Finally, let's look at what you can do once you know you are under an enemy attack.

What to Do When the Enemy Attacks

When you first sense you are under enemy attack, go immediately back to the basics.

1. Check to see that you are proclaiming the Lordship of Jesus in every area of your life.

Sometimes we exclude Him without realizing it. Say, "Jesus is Lord over my mind." "Jesus is Lord over my finances." "Jesus is Lord over my relationships." Specifically name the area the enemy is threatening.

2. Saturate yourself with God's Word.

Specifically, read promises from God concerning this specific type of enemy attack, and speak them aloud in the face of your circumstances. Go back to the list of pitfalls and refer to the Scriptures in areas that apply to you.

Scripture also gives us a concise procedure to follow in any spiritual warfare in Ephesians 6, which tells us to "put on the whole armor of God, that you may be able to stand against the wiles of the devil" (vv. 10–20).

In his book *What You Need to Know about Spiritual Warfare in 12 Lessons*, Max Anders applies the parts of the armor directly to our lives and spiritual warfare. Check each piece of armor which follows, vowing to make this application to your life:

_____ "I accept the truth of the Bible and choose to follow it with integrity. I put on the Belt of Truth."

_____ "I will not harbor known sin, and I will strive to live like Christ. I put on the Breastplate of Righteousness."

_____ "I believe the promises of God and count on them to be true for me. I put on the Shoes of the Gospel of Peace."

_____ "Whenever I feel like doubting or sinning or quitting, I will reject those thoughts and feelings and declare to myself the truth. I will put on the Shield of Faith."

_____ "I rest my hope in the future and live in this world according to the value system of the next. I put on the Helmet of Salvation."

_____ "I will use the Scriptures specifically in life's situations to fend off attacks of the enemy and put him to flight. I will buckle on the Sword of the Spirit."[4]

If you have checked these statements, you have put on God's armor to defeat the enemy. You might want to review them every so often to make sure that you are still fully equipped to defeat the devil. And always remember: "He who is in [me] is greater than he who is in the world" (1 John 4:4).

3. Be much in prayer.

Ask God to reveal the truth of your situation to you. Ask Him for guidance, protection, and strength for whatever you are facing. Remember: there is no unity in the realm of darkness. That's why the two weakest Christians have more power, if they are in unity, than all the power of hell.

4. Continue to praise God in the midst of whatever is happening.

Remember that God inhabits the praises of His people, and you will always be safe in His presence.

5. Ask God to show you if there are any points of obedience you have not taken.

Lack of obedience always opens us up to enemy attack. Stop now and check to make sure you are still living in obedience. Place a check beside those that are still a part of your life:

I am living in obedience by . . .

_____ taking charge of my mind;

_____ saying no to sexual immorality;

_____ renouncing the occult;

_____ cleaning out my house;

_____ taking care of my body;

_____ watching what I say.

If there is an area where you are weak, take that to the Lord by writing a prayer below, asking Him to help you grow in this area:

6. Fast and pray.

This is a powerful weapon for breaking down enemy strongholds that have been erected against you.

7. Resist Satan.

Don't run from the enemy, but instead face him with all the spiritual weapons at your disposal. Because Jesus is in you, you have full authority and power over Satan.

8. Rest in the Lord.

Once you have done all you know to do, be still and know that Jesus is the victor and the battle is the Lord's. Gain strength in that knowledge.

When the heat is on and the battle is raging, know that as long as you are standing strong in the Lord, you won't be shot down or burned up by your circumstances. Think in terms of God's power, not your own weakness. Don't give the devil the pleasure of seeing you give up.

Attributes of God to Hold On to When You Are Involved in Spiritual Warfare

Write the passages of Scripture that substantiate the attributes of God in the spaces below.

God will forgive me: 1 John 1:9

God will comfort me: Psalm 34:17–18

God will bless me: Romans 10:12–13

God will guide me: Isaiah 58:11

God is powerful: Isaiah 14:27

35

STANDING STRONG WHEN YOUR PRAYERS HAVEN'T BEEN ANSWERED

Duane Miller knows how difficult it is to stand strong when fervent prayers go unanswered. He was the senior pastor at First Baptist Church in Brenham, Texas, when his faith was tested in a way that led this minister into a deep, dark valley of despair.

On Sunday, January 14, 1990, he preached the first service, had to shorten his sermon by many minutes for the second service, and was unable to preach the Sunday evening service at all. Only days later his voice was almost completely gone. *It's just the flu,* Duane thought. During the next ten days he suffered from a devastating flu—and during the entire time his throat felt like sandpaper.

Soon his voice was reduced to a slight, raspy whisper. Duane explains the feeling this way: "Wrap both hands around your throat with your thumbs nestled under your chin. Squeeze in with your thumbs and lift up with your fingers. Notice how you suddenly have to swallow."[1] Duane continually experienced this strangling sensation. But worst of all he could hardly breathe.

Doctor after doctor tried to diagnose Duane's problem—and cure his condition—but no one could come up with an answer. Finally, they said he would have to take a six-month leave of absence from his ministry.

During that time Duane felt like Van Cliburn with his hands cut off: "You can still hear the music, but you can't play it." His physical ability to speak had been taken, but his gift of teaching remained. Sermon ideas and passages came into his mind, but he could no longer express them.

And after six months of rest, his voice was still a slight, raspy whisper.

The doctors admitted that Duane might never be able to preach again. This realization plunged Duane into a long, dark tunnel with a twist in the middle that blocked any light. His prayers for healing had remained unanswered; he knew he had to resign his position as senior pastor.

Yet God is God when things are bad as well as when they are good, when it is dark as well as when it is light. Sometimes the darkness around us is not a darkness of death but rather a darkness like in a womb, where we are growing and being made ready for birth. We just don't know it. As a child in the womb knows nothing of the world waiting for him, so we do not realize the greatness of God's purpose for us. The Bible says, "I will give you the treasures of darkness" (Isa. 45:3). Certain valuable experiences in the Lord can *only* be found in the dark times.

How to Grow in the Dark

So what do you do when you've believed and praised and prayed but are still disillusioned and afraid your dreams and hopes are gone?

First of all, don't be consumed with guilt. Don't feel that this is your fault and therefore God won't answer your prayer. However, if your prayers are unanswered because of sin, confess it, stop doing it, and pray. God will turn things around.

In his book *What You Need to Know about Spiritual Warfare in 12 Lessons,* Max Anders gives five reasons God may delay answering our prayers. Check the statement below that might apply to your situation if your prayers have not been answered for yourself, your family, or your friends:

_____ The timing is not right. He may answer the prayer—later.

_____ The request needs to be clarified. (Anders says, "When the answer comes, God wants us to be able to recognize it. Often we don't recognize an answer because we did not crystallize the request in our own minds.")

_____ God might want to intensify our expectations and to call attention to the fact that it was He who answered, not just good luck or natural consequences.

_____ God wants to deepen our understanding of Him and His word.

_____ He is drawing us into a deeper relationship with Him.
(Anders says, "Things that come easily are often taken
lightly. God does not want prayer to be taken lightly.
Therefore, answers to prayer do not always come readily.")[2]

If you checked one of the previous statements, God may be going to answer your prayer in His own time, which may be next week or next month or next year.

Second, allow no situation to make you turn your back on Him. Know that He sees where you are, He has not forgotten you, and He will sustain you through it.

Duane Miller uses Matthew 14 (Peter's walking on water) in his book, *Out of the Silence*, when he talks about unanswered prayer. He says, "When the Savior comes to rescue us from the storm, we must let go of the boat and keep our eyes on Him, even when the circumstances of the storm are still swirling around us! Often, in the midst of the storm, we will hear Jesus calling to us and begin to respond, only to be stopped when we realize the storm is still raging. The contrary wind didn't cease until Peter had reached Jesus and they both had returned to the boat. Don't miss this principle: When you have prayed for help and the storm seems as if it will never end, don't give up and sink; just keep walking toward Jesus.

"Don't let the observation of unchanged circumstances defeat you. I AM has called and is in control. Keep walking!

"Notice, too," he says, "that when Peter began to sink, all Jesus had to do was reach down to pull him up. Principle? Not only are we always within His sight, but we are always within arm's length of the Lord."[3]

Part of standing strong in times of unanswered prayer is waiting, and waiting produces patience. The Bible says, "By your patience possess your souls" (Luke 21:19). When you are patient, you're able to take control of your very being and place yourself in God's hands. He, then, is in control whether it is night or day in your soul.

Since we have no choice but to wait, our attitude makes a lot of difference. We can either shake our fist at God and scream, "Why me?" Or we can open up our hearts to God and pray, "Lord, change this situation. Perfect Your life in me as I wait on You. Help me to do the right thing, and let it all work out for my greatest need."

Duane Miller knows how important attitude is at times when your prayers remain unanswered. He says, "I would love to tell you that throughout these difficult years I stood my ground as a mighty man of faith . . . The only problem is, if I told you those things, I would be lying. There were days when I cried out to the Lord, 'What are you doing, God? Why don't You help me?'

"I didn't even want to go to church anymore. I couldn't sing, so worship was more frustrating than joyful. I listened to a great sermon, which, more than anything else, reminded me of my own inability to preach . . .

"Here was the real danger of my situation: The enemy was trying to turn my illness into a stronghold. His first plan was to alienate me from the body of Christ."[4]

And soon financial pressures overburdened Duane. First, his job as a private investigator, helping a federal agency to find property that had been fraudulently transferred, was terminated. Then the insurance agency that had been paying for his treatment said he was no longer eligible for coverage, and a month later the company that had been paying his disability checks also cancelled his coverage.

And the commission that Duane felt God had given him—to minister to God's people—was not possible. "The desire to preach never left my soul," Duane Miller says. "Even so, preaching was a practical impossibility. I had to let go of it."[5]

To survive, he had to discover an entirely new strength. And at that moment, Cherie Young asked him to lead the fall retreat for the Catacombs class at First Baptist Church in Houston. Duane had been on the staff there and taught the class for years before he became the senior pastor at Brenham. Now that he had moved back to Houston, the class wanted him to lead this retreat, even if he could hardly be heard.

It was a bittersweet experience. Duane got a taste of teaching again, but also realized how limited he was. He could only speak for about ten minutes at a time before his throat went into spasms.

Yet when the teacher of the Catacombs class had to step down for personal reasons in 1992, Cherie Young asked him to replace the man. She explained that he could teach by using a microphone to amplify his whisper.

Teaching this class, Duane says, is what helped to keep him sane. "In the midst of bad report after bad report, and financial blow after financial blow, at least I could lose myself in God's Word and in explaining Scripture to others."[6]

And the class increased as he continued to teach. But the price Duane had to pay also increased. "When I spoke for one hour on Sunday, I lit a painful fire in the back of my throat that didn't go out until late Tuesday or early Wednesday. Unfortunately the doctor's prediction that my situation would eventually grow worse was coming true."[7]

At this moment God sent another blessing: the desire to write. Duane decided to develop a newsletter, *Practical Christianity*, to give Christians thoughts about how they could grow in their faith. Finally, his energies were being used to serve God.

His father-in-law predicted, "God sent you to Brenham to deliver a message, and that message was given. He stopped your voice to move you back to Houston and to bring glory to Himself. Ultimately, the new ministry God is going to give to you will far outshine your earlier one."[8]

Finally, one Sunday morning Duane prayed this prayer of surrender: "Okay, God, if you choose to change things, which I know you can do—great! But until then, I'm going to accept things as they are and live accordingly."[9]

Duane says, "To all those who are weighed down by the burden of life, I encourage you, find something to do to serve God. When the great missionary, Hudson Taylor, was completely bedridden, he had someone tape a map to the wall so he could intercede for God's work. He couldn't preach a sermon, he couldn't pass out food, he couldn't even lift a pencil to write an encouraging letter, but he could pray."[10]

You may have to wait for God to move, but you don't have to sit twiddling your thumbs until it happens. The best way to sustain a good attitude while you wait is to spend much time in praise and worship of God. Write a prayer of praise in the following space, praising Him in the midst of this situation. Then admit that you are discouraged from the waiting and feel you are losing the strength to fight.

Don't stop praying even if you've been doing it for a long time and it seems as if God must not be listening.

"Though God often asks His people to walk through many deserts, He occasionally graces their journey with a fragrant flower," Duane says. Duane explains his analogy this way: People think of deserts as vast spaces of blowing sand, but here and there God has planted a desert flower. And that's also true, he says, when we're going through a period of unanswered prayer.[11]

The first flower was the change in his wife, Joylene. When she had to go to work, Duane felt guilty. He was the breadwinner. But as the months progressed he noticed how Joylene's success at her job gave her increased confidence. God had also provided a new home for them when they moved back to Houston, a home that was beyond their meager means at the time. For some unexplainable reason—unless you put God into the equation— the owner accepted an offer that was 40 percent of his asking price.

These occurrences reminded Duane of Isaiah 9:2: "The people who walked in darkness have seen a great light; Those who dwelt in the land of the shadow of death, upon them a light has shined."

Scripture to Consider As You Are
Walking Through a Time of Unanswered Prayer

Matthew 14:22–33

James 5:13–16

Philippians 4:6–7

Matthew 21:22

1 Peter 3:12

36

STANDING STRONG WHEN YOUR PRAYERS HAVE BEEN ANSWERED

Duane Miller also learned how to stand strong when prayers are answered. After eighteen months of going to doctor after doctor, Duane Miller's problem had still not been diagnosed. So one of his doctors decided to videotape his throat and take the video to an international symposium in Switzerland.

The incredible amount of scar tissue that had formed on Duane's vocal cords from his flu-like illness was so rare that the video was shown to the entire symposium, rather than just a few doctors. Duane was using the false cords in his throat (the small bumps on each side of his throat, very near the bottom) to speak, which is what these false cords do when someone gets laryngitis. But these cords do not sustain speech over a long period of time.

For several days the specialists at this symposium discussed Duane's condition. And instead of a new treatment, they decided that Duane had little chance of recovery. Zero, in fact. They said that he would be permanently disabled. "You will become completely mute," the doctor reported to Duane. "Probably late '94 or early '95. By then you won't be able to make a sound."[1]

Shortly before Christmas 1992, the doctor's prediction began to be true. Duane's throat became steadily worse.

He awoke one Sunday morning in January of 1993 and had great difficulty speaking at all. He knew he couldn't teach the Catacombs class that morning. But no substitute could be found. Ironically the lesson was on God's miraculous and faithful provision for His people and His ability to heal! This lesson was from the Southern Baptist Convention Bible Book Series, which is scheduled seven years in advance, so this lesson went on the calendar back in 1986.

Duane told the class that the statement that the Israelites wandered in the wilderness for forty years just wasn't true. "They weren't wandering," he said. "Sure, they may not have known where they were going, but they were following the cloud by day and the pillar of fire by night, both of which represented God's presence. They weren't *wandering*, they were *following*. And God most certainly knew where He was going and where He was taking them. He was never lost and He was never confused. There was a purpose in every step they took, because God always has a purpose in everything He does, whether we understand it or not.

"There are times when we follow God and we feel like we are following aimlessly. But when we are following God, there is no aimlessness in it."[2]

You might wonder how Duane could make such a statement when his own condition was so hopeless. But Duane had never lost his belief in the sovereignty of God

That Sunday morning Duane continued his teaching with an explanation of Psalm 103: "God heals all my diseases" (v. 3). Sometimes God heals our sickness, Duane said, by loaning us extra life, and sometimes He chooses to heal by bringing the person home to Him. That morning Duane made it very clear that God is not a genie-in-a-bottle to answer our prayers or an apathetic bystander who no longer gets involved.

Then Duane asked the Catacombs class, "What happens when we put God in a box and say He doesn't heal anymore?" He paused for a moment for emphasis, then said, "He kicks all the walls down!"

How could Duane continue to tell the class that God heals—when he hadn't been healed? Only because God's Word said it.

At this point the pain in Duane's throat became almost unbearable. He had been teaching for over twenty minutes and was hardly able to make his usual raspy sound.

Yet he went on to read verse four: "He redeems my life from the pit."

When Duane spoke the word *pit*, the hands that had been choking his throat for over three years suddenly let go. Seconds before he had felt like he was suffocating. Now he could breathe naturally.

He heard a gasp from the members of the class, and then he realized what had happened. His voice had returned, just as strong as ever!

"The presence of the Holy Spirit was so palpable that everyone's nerve endings felt exposed," Duane says. "It was as if we were lifted to a higher existence and you could take hold of the Spirit with your bare hands."

At first he was afraid this might not last, but the natural sensation in his throat told him: "I had a new throat! . . . What was dead had literally and stunningly come back to life."

Duane tried to continue with the lesson, but finally his tears of joy made further talk impossible.

"Let me just wrap it up by saying this," he told the class. "I know that wherever you are in your life and whatever is going on with you, and however deep the pit or however high the mountain, God is there! He is there! And as you have lived with me these last years—would you believe, three years this Sunday, three years today since I preached my last sermon . . ."

This realization bought such joy that Duane could no longer continue. The worship leader of the class stood up and began to sing the Doxology—and the rest of the class joined in. "Praise God from whom all blessings flow . . . Praise Father, Son, and Holy Ghost!"[3]

Over two-hundred members of the Catacombs class witnessed Duane's healing on January 17, 1993, and the entire congregation of that church heard him speak later that morning during the Sunday service. But God had yet another surprise in store. The Catacomb's classes were taped each week, so this miracle was recorded.

These tapes were quickly passed among residents of Houston and then began to spread around the country—and the world. Dr. James Dobson heard one and asked Duane to appear on the radio broadcast of *Focus on the Family.*

The light that began to return when Duane Miller's prayers were unanswered now shone brightly when a miracle was God's answer.

Duane says, "My story is not one of overcoming faith. I did nothing, I believed nothing, I achieved nothing, to warrant God's incredible touch. Instead, my story is of the dynamic power and grace of a merciful, loving, and sovereign God."[4]

Yet how quickly we sometimes forget God's blessings.

How Quickly We Forget

The truth about human flesh is that when we come to a place of comfort, we tend to forget God. As I read through the Old Testament from beginning to end, what impressed me the most was how the Israelites sought God, repented, and prayed when things were bad, and God heard and answered their prayers. Once everything was going well, they forgot where they had come from, forgot what God had done, and started living their own way again. In good times, they forgot God and sinned—time and again.

You and I are no different. How many of us can say that we pray as fervently when all is well as we do when all hell is breaking loose? Not many, I'm sure. Yet the Bible says, "Let him who thinks he stands take heed lest he fall" (1 Cor. 10:12). When things are going well, beware!

Mary Anne explained to me, "When we enter the promised land, we don't think about the giants; we thing about the milk and honey, about how good this feels and what life will be like now that we've been set free and are being renewed. We know that evil lurks about, but we don't want to think about that now, not when things are good. That's why when an attack comes, we are so unprepared. When we enter the promised land, we need to know there are giants we must face."

"Who are these giants?" I asked.

Mary Anne named certain enemies that were in the promised land as described in the book of Exodus. She said she found that the meanings of their names correlated with areas of our flesh, such as fear, confusion, discouragement, pride, rebelliousness, and condemnation. These were exactly the ones that threatened me when I came into my time of restoration, and the ones we must be ready to battle, even in time of peace.

Take a moment now to inventory your spiritual life by reviewing the building blocks that strengthen our relationship with God. Check the statements below that apply to you:

_____ "I have been studying the Word of God regularly."

_____ "I have been keeping a daily prayer time."

_____ "I have been thanking God for His blessings and praising Him for being my Savior and Creator."

_____ "I have been regularly confessing my sins to the Lord."

_____ "I have been continuing to forgive those who hurt me."

If you checked the above statements, your foundation in the Lord is strong. You are walking in God's will for your life.

Keep It Written in Stone

Years ago Pastor Jack instructed each family unit in our church, single or married, to go out and find a rock large enough to write the words, "As for me and my house, we will serve the LORD" (Josh. 24:15), and then put it in a prominent place in their home.

A friend of mine who was building an addition onto her house did something similar. When the foundation was being set, she took a magic marker and inscribed the same verse on the cement and the date. From that time forward her commitment to the Lord was written on the foundation of their home, a good rock upon which to build.

I'm giving you an assignment. Go find yourself a decent-sized rock, print that Scripture on it with an indelible marker, and place it in the heart of your home.

Then also write your name in the space below to commemorate that goal here:

But you, _____, must continue in the things which you have learned and been assured of, knowing from whom you have learned them. (2 Tim. 3:14)

Don't ever be fooled into believing that when all is going well, you don't need to read, pray, praise, and obey as carefully as you did before. Resolve to stand strong in the Lord, even when your prayers have been answered, and you will live safely in the promised land of God's restoration.

Scriptures to Consider When Your
Prayers Have Been Answered

On Sunday, January 17, 1993, Duane Miller was teaching from the Scriptures below. Read the passages and then note the verses that are most significant to you.

Psalm 68

Psalm 103

37

BECOMING ALL GOD MADE YOU TO BE

As I mentioned in chapter 1, at my dad's funeral we each told a fond recollection of him. One of my memories was of my dad sitting at the dining room table with my children after they came home from school every day. He would tell them exciting stories about his life as a young cowboy in Wyoming. And he always told them with exactly the same words! (Senility was not a problem for Dad.) As I watched them each day I realized that he was passing on a wonderful heritage about life on the prairie, an exciting adventure where death was always closer than many of us ever experience.

These moments would never have happened if I hadn't forgiven my dad. Certainly I would never have asked him to live with us for six years if the bitterness I had toward my parents hadn't been resolved. And my children would never have known their grandpa in this intimate way, which was so very enriching for them.

In the days ahead you will also experience blessings you might never have known if you hadn't walked this journey to emotional health.

You've just gone through the Seven Steps, and if you have taken even one step in each area, there are bound to be noticeable positive changes in your life. You may not see as many as you'd like yet, but don't give up. You will. God promises that "He who has begun a good work in you will complete it until the day of Jesus Christ" (Phil. 1:6).

I'm going to assume that if you've read this far, you've already decided you want all God has for you. When this desire turns into a hunger for more of the Lord that can only be completely satisfied when you are in His presence, then you are on your way to becoming all you can be.

You will remember that my definition of emotional health is having total peace about who you are, what you're doing, and where you're going, both individually and in relationship to those around you. It's feeling totally at peace about the past, the present, and the future of your life. It's knowing that you're in line with God's ultimate purpose for you—and being fulfilled in that.

Now it's time to take a final inventory. In the space below list the moments since you have begun this workbook that have given you peace and a sense of well-being:

Now think about the moments during this time that made you feel agitated and uneasy. List those moments below:

Finally, think about the future. What possible events in the future would make you happy and at peace? List them below:

What events in the future might make you afraid and uneasy? List them below:

Now go back to the first inventory you took in chapter 1. Compare that inventory to this one. How are the moments you listed there different from the ones you listed above?

How are the moments in chapter 1 similar to the ones you listed on the previous page?

When you did your inventory in chapter 1, what were the two most important events (the ones that made you feel afraid and uneasy) in the past, present, and future that you said you needed to deal with as you read this book? Have you dealt with them?

If not, go back to the chapters that discussed these issues and work through them again. If you have dealt with these issues in the book, congratulations. You have taken important steps in your emotional and spiritual journey.

Now that you are on the road to emotional health, you need to remain sensitive to what is currently happening inside you.

Staying Emotionally Current

Because your focus is so much on the Lord and living His ways, you can deal with your emotions as they surface.

Every one of us has countless tears buried inside. The Bible says, "To everything there is a season . . . A time to weep, and a time to laugh; a time to mourn, and a time to dance" (Eccl. 3:1,4).

We would be wise to remember that.

Our emotions don't have to rule our lives, but we shouldn't ignore them either. Listen to what you are feeling and ask God to help you identify and deal with it. Keep yourself emotionally current at all times.

Remembering the Truth About Yourself

We all want to be somebody. The truth is, God created each one of us to be somebody and no life is an accident or unwanted in His eyes. He has given us each a distinct purpose or calling. It is not humility to deny the Lord's extraordinary qualities in us, it's low self-esteem.

High self-esteem means seeing yourself as God sees you, and recognizing that you are a unique person in whom He has placed specific gifts, talents, and purpose unlike anyone else.

The Bible says, "A house divided against itself will fall" (Luke 11:17 NIV). This means that a person who has turned against himself won't make it. Much of your emotional pain may be caused by believing untrue things about yourself. Many times God was the only One who believed in me, but that was enough. I know now that because I believe in Him and He believes in me, I can make it. So can you!

Now take a final inventory of who you are at this moment, after having completed this workbook.

Think about who you are. Write a description in the space below. (Be sure to include who you are spiritually and emotionally.)

Do you have total peace about who you are? _____ yes; _____ no.

If not, mention below the ways you would like to change:

Now think about who you are in relationship to those around you. Write that description in the space below:

Are you at peace with who you are in relationship to others?
_____ yes; _____ no.

If not, mention below the ways you could change who you are in relationship to others:

Think about what you're doing. Look back at the time since you began this workbook. Mention the activities that seemed to consume most of your time in the space below:

Are you at peace with what you are doing? _____ yes; _____ no.

If not, mention below the ways you might want to change what you are doing in the future:

Now think about what you are doing and how it affects those around you. Write that description in the space below:

Are you at peace with how what you are doing affects those around you? _____ yes; _____ no.

If not, mention below the ways you might change what you are doing in relationship to others:

Finally, think about where you are going. Write a description below of what you anticipate in the future:

Are you at peace with where you are going? _____ yes; _____ no.

If not, mention below the ways you might want to change your future:

Now think about where you are going in relationship to those around you. Write a description in the space below:

Are you at peace with where you are going? _____ yes; _____ no.

If not, mention how you might change that in the space below:

Again go back to chapter 1, to the second inventory and compare it to this one.

Have you made any changes in the three areas: who you are, who you are in relationship to those around you, and what you are doing? If so, list those below.

Who you are:

Who you are in relationship to those around you:

What you are doing:

Have you identified other areas you want to change in the future? If so, list them here:

Now write a prayer in the space below, asking God to help you make those changes in the days ahead. Thank Him for His guidance during your walk through this workbook—and ask Him to be with you in the future:

If at any time you become overwhelmed by how much you think you have to do to arrive at emotional wholeness, or if you have doubts about whether you can do all that's necessary, then you need to remind yourself that it is the Holy Spirit who accomplishes wholeness in you. Let Him do it. Tell God that you want His ways to become your ways so that you can become all He wants you to be.

YOUR PRAYER JOURNAL

Your Prayer Journal

Your Prayer Journal

YOUR PRAYER JOURNAL

Your Prayer Journal

Your Prayer Journal

YOUR PRAYER JOURNAL

Your Prayer Journal

Your Prayer Journal

YOUR PRAYER JOURNAL

Your Prayer Journal

YOUR PRAYER JOURNAL

Your Prayer Journal

YOUR PRAYER JOURNAL

YOUR PRAYER JOURNAL

YOUR PRAYER JOURNAL

Your Prayer Journal

Your Prayer Journal

NOTES

CHAPTER 2

1. Charles W. Colson, *Born Again* (Grand Rapids, MI: Fleming H. Revell Co., a div. of Baker, 1996), 113–114.

2. Charles W. Colson, *Born Again* (Grand Rapids, MI: Fleming H. Revell Co., a div. of Baker, 1996), 113–114.

3. Ibid., 223.

4. Ibid., 249.

5. Ibid., 139.

CHAPTER 3

1. Charles W. Colson, *Born Again*, 260.

2. Ibid., 260–261

3. Ibid., 338–340.

CHAPTER 6

1. Rich Buhler, *Pain and Pretending* (Nashville: Thomas Nelson, 1991), 57.

2. Ibid., 161.

3. Ibid., 162.

4. Ibid., 168-169.

5. Frank Minirth, Paul Meier, Stephen Arterburn, *The Complete Life Encyclopedia* (Nashville: Thomas Nelson, 1995), 514–515.

CHAPTER 9

1. Kenneth H. Cooper, *Regaining the Power of Youth at Any Age* (Nashville: Thomas Nelson, 1998).

2. Ibid.

3. Ibid.

CHAPTER 12

1. *The American Heritage Dictionary*, Second College Edition (Boston: Houghton Mifflin Company, 1982), 967.

2. Ibid.

3. Christopher L. Coppernoll, *soul 2 soul* (Nashville: Word Publishing, 1998), 162–164.

4. Max Anders, *What You Need to Know about Spiritual Warfare in 12 Lessons* (Nashville: Thomas Nelson, 1997), 9–10.

5. Christopher L. Coppernoll, *soul 2 soul*, 164.

CHAPTER 13

1. Gary Smalley & John Trent, *The Gift of the Blessing* (Nashville: Thomas Nelson, 1993), 178–180.

2. Ibid., 183–184.

3. Ibid., 18.

4. Ibid., 49.

5. Ibid., 67,69.

6. Ibid., 100–106.

7. Ibid., 13–15.

CHAPTER 14

1. Lori Graham Bakker, *More Than I Could Ever Ask* (Nashville: Thomas Nelson, 2000), 175.

2. Ibid., 169.

CHAPTER 15

1. Lori Graham Bakker, *More Than I Could*, 304-305.

2. Ibid., 306–307.

CHAPTER 17

1. Lori Graham Bakker, *More Than I Could*, 25.

2. Ibid., 212.

CHAPTER 19

1. C. S. Lewis, *The Screwtape Letters* (New York: Macmillan Publishing Co., 1961), xi.

CHAPTER 22

1. Dr. Chris Thurman, *The Lies We Believe* (Nashville: Thomas Nelson, 1989), 55.

CHAPTER 27

1. *Webster's New World Dictionary,* Third Edition (New York: Simon & Schuster, 1997), 1003.

1. Dr. David Stoop, *Living with a Perfectionist* (Nashville: Thomas Nelson, 1987).

CHAPTER 29

1. Thomas O. Chisholm, *Great is Thy Faithfulness* © 1923. Renewal 1951 by Hope Publishing Co., Carol Stream, IL 60188. All rights reserved. Used by permission.

CHAPTER 31

1. Oswald Chambers, *My Utmost for His Highest: An Updated Edition in Today's Language*, James Reimann (Nashville: Thomas Nelson, 1992), 5/16.
2. Ibid., 6/27.

CHAPTER 33

1. Kenneth H. Cooper, *Regaining the Power of Youth*, 145.
2. Ibid., 146.

CHAPTER 34

1. Maisie Sparks, *101 Things the Devil Can't Do* (Nashville: Thomas Nelson, 2000), 1.
2. Ibid., 2
3. Ibid., 57.
4. Max Anders, *What You Need to Know About Spiritual Warfare*, 161.

CHAPTER 35

1. Duane Miller, *Out of the Silence* (Nashville: Thomas Nelson, Inc., 1996), 6.
2. Max Anders, *What You Need to Know About Spiritual Warfare*, 119.
3. Duane Miller, *Out of the Silence*, 191.
4. Ibid., 76.
5. Ibid., 63.
6. Ibid., 96.
7. Ibid.
8. Ibid., 101.
9. Ibid., 102.
10. Ibid., 98.
11. Ibid., 49.

CHAPTER 36

1. Duane Miller, *Out of the Silence*, 83.
2. Ibid., 118.
3. Ibid., 118–128.
4. Ibid., 7.

About the Author

STORMIE OMARTIAN is a popular writer, accomplished songwriter, speaker, and author. Her other books include the bestsellers *Praying God's Will for Your Life*; *Praying God's Will for Your Life Workbook and Journal*; *Lord, I Want to Be Whole* (Gold Medallion winner); *The Power of a Praying Husband* (Gold Medallion winner); *The Power of a Praying Wife*; and *The Power of a Praying Parent.*

A popular media guest, Stormie has appeared on numerous radio and television programs, including *The 700 Club*, *Parent Talk*, *Homelife*, *Crosstalk*, and *Today's Issues*. Stormie speaks all over the United States in churches, at women's retreats, and at conferences. For over twenty years Stormie has been encouraging women to pray for their families. She desires to help others become all that God created them to be, to establish strong family bonds and marriages, and to be instruments of God's love.

Stormie has been married to Grammy-winning record producer Michael Omartian for twenty-nine years. They have three grown children: Christopher, Amanda, and John David.

You can contact Stormie through her Web site: www.stormieomartian.com

The Power of Prayer *and* Scripture in
Emotional Healing

Lord,
I Want to Be Whole

Stormie Omartian

Author of the Bestseller **The Power of a Praying Wife**

"LORD, I WANT TO BE WHOLE."

These words are the heart-cry of many Christians who, in spite of their relationship with the Lord, find themselves dealing with overwhelming anger, guilt, depression—or perhaps the nagging feeling that something inside them just is not right.

In *Lord, I Want to Be Whole,* Stormie Omartian shares the principles she learned during her struggle for wholeness and real and lasting peace. What Stormie offers is not a formula for a quick fix but a positive approach that is both spiritual and practical. Her advice and encouragement will help you find—and keep—wholeness in all areas of your life.

ISBN: 0-7852-6703-4

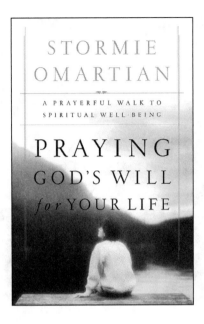

"GOD, IF YOU HAVE A WILL FOR MY LIFE, I need to know what it is and what to do about it."

Even before she became a Christian, Stormie Omartian prayed those words. In the months that followed, God answered her in ways that she didn't believe possible. As God unfolded His plan for her life, she began to understand what it meant to live in God's will. And she found that she could share her discovery with other people.

Praying God's Will for Your Life is not a book about finding the right person to marry or deciding on a career. It is a book about a way of life and a heart attitude that are God's will for everyone who knows Him. That way of life encompasses three important components:

- An intimate relationship with God

- A solid foundation in God's truth

- A commitment to obedience

ISBN: 0-7852-6645-3

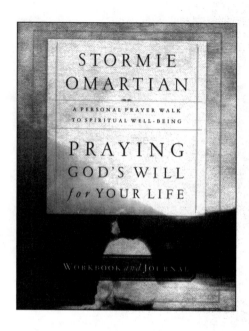

In *Praying God's Will for Your Life Workbook and Journal,* the focus is uniquely on you—your past, your present, and your future. Each week, for twenty-two weeks, you will work through interactive questions and thought-provoking Scriptures that will enable you to deepen your walk with the Lord, just as Stormie deepened her own relationship with the Father. You will read inspiring stories of women like yourself who have grown by following the steps in this process. You will journal your thoughts through prayers to your Heavenly Father. This path will become your path. And the spiritual growth your own spiritual growth—a diary of your own walk with God.

This easy-to-use workbook serves as an excellent guide for either personal devotions or group study. Use it as a stand-alone Bible study or as a companion to Stormie's book, *Praying God's Will for Your Life.*

ISBN: 0-7852-6407-8